Contents

A note on the text and acknowledgments

La Conspiration was first published by Gallimard in the autumn of 1938. References in this guide, included after the quotations in **bold** typeface, e.g. (**30**), are to the paperback Gallimard 'Folio' edition, first published in 1973, and to the 1996 printing of that edition. It might be helpful to readers of any 'Folio' text dated earlier (with more representational artwork on the cover than the painting by Seiwert) to point out that line 28 of page 219—'-raderie n'est au-dessus de la Révolution et qu'il y avait'—is inadvertently duplicated as line 3 of the following page. In order that this part of the heated exchange between Rosenthal, Laforgue and Pluvinage be fully understood, for it makes little sense unless the change of speaker is indicated, here is the missing line: 'circonstances aussi graves. Pluvinage lui dit qu'il avait'.

Details of Nizan's other principal works are given in the Bibliography.

I am indebted to Rosie Jones for her help in the preparation of the manuscript for publication, and to Harry Guest and John Fletcher for their comments.

John Flower   Canterbury, October 1999

Introduction

Writing to order

On a number of occasions, François Mauriac observed that he was not a Catholic novelist but a Catholic who, by chance, happened also to be a novelist. Quite how useful or indeed possible such a distinction is has always been a matter for discussion, especially when, for example, Mauriac seems to have had no hesitation in calling fellow Catholic writers, such as Georges Bernanos or Graham Greene, 'romanciers catholiques'. The issue is not a simple one. It is difficult to imagine how people, and especially creative artists, whose lives are fundamentally expressions or reflections of personal faith, can do other than have that faith permeate their work. This is not to say that in the case of Catholic writers the only subjects about which they may write with impunity will be exemplary and illustrative of their religious conviction: priests, saints, martyrs and so on. Few, as Sartre recognized, have achieved the success, in French literature at least, of Bernanos with his *Journal d'un curé de campagne*, or of Dostoievski; that is to say, their works, while without question deeply influenced by their faith, appeal powerfully to and can be appreciated by the non-believer. Rather, this faith will appear indirectly, obliquely, and indeed can apparently be absent altogether, creating what some critics used to define in the case of Mauriac as an 'indirect apology'. It may even be that evil will be given prominence, thereby creating a negative, hollow view of human nature about which the reader is left to draw his own conclusions. We should not forget that, for the Catholic, man is, after all, a flawed, fallen creature. And, albeit in a slightly different context, did Gide not once observe that for any novel to be successful the collaboration of the devil was necessary?

Considerations such as these are not irrelevant to the study of writers whose works reflect or are driven by political ideology and, in the modern period, by Communism in particular. Again Sartre, in *Qu'est-ce que la littérature?*, has not been alone in pointing to the parallel between two faiths which demand unflinching obedience. And does not Carré, in *La Conspiration*, explain to the hesitant Régnier that the reason why the Catholic church fears Communism is because the latter is also constructed around 'la certitude d'une victoire absolument totale'(**211**)? But, unlike Catholic writers, most if not all of those who have embraced and set out to extol the virtues of Communism in their works have, sooner or later, been obliged to face up to the issue of directives or prescriptions dictated by the Party's cultural policy-makers or their national representatives.

Since the early twentieth century this issue has had three phases in France. During the 1920s, favourable echoes and accounts of cultural policy in the Soviet Union were relayed through the columns of periodicals like Henri Barbusse's *Clarté* and *Monde*, or in the daily paper *L'Humanité*. While there was no overt attempt to draw up a specific cultural policy by the Party in France at this time, increasing ideological orthodoxy and discipline in the Soviet Union found its expression through the Association of Proletarian Writers (RAPP) which encouraged the production of works extolling the virtues and success of the Revolution. The Association's high point was an international congress at Kharkov in 1930, when all failures to follow the Party line were openly challenged and condemned. Paul Nizan (born 1905) was one of those present and, as we shall see, was charged with the task of disciplining Barbusse and *Monde*. But increasing political orthodoxy brought disillusionment and disappointment, and support for the Party on an international scale began to fall dramatically. In France at the general election of 1928, thirteen out of twenty-eight Communist deputies lost their seats, and by 1933 national support for the Party had fallen to only a quarter of what it had been seven or eight years earlier. Such a state of affairs could not be allowed to continue if the Party were to remain a significant political force. New policies of openness and collaboration were introduced which, in France, would lead to the creation in 1935 of the Popular Front. Again cultural policy took its direction from political change. In 1932, the RAPP was replaced by the Union of Soviet Writers, and the same year saw the foundation in France of the Association des écrivains et artistes révolutionnaires (AEAR) and its monthly review *Commune*. This was the main channel through which new orthodoxy for art and literature would be broadcast; its new formula was that of socialist realism.[1]

The first statements in French about this form of writing appeared in the translation of an article by Vladimir Kirpotin in October 1933 in *La Littérature internationale*. The initial impression the article creates is of a broad liberalisation and a recognition of the dangers of 'writing to order' and of schematization: 'on ne peut transformer le mot d'ordre du réalisme socialiste en recette schématique'. But a 'mot d'ordre' there is and it quickly becomes apparent that certain directives remain.

> Lorsque nous parlons de réalisme socialiste, nous avons en vue ce qui dans l'art représente le monde objectif, non seulement dans ses détails superficiels ou voire même dans des détails essentiels, mais encore dans toutes les circonstances fondamentales, et à l'aide de caractères typiques essentiels. Nous avons en vue ce qui représente la vie véridique avec ses côtés négatifs et positifs, avec l'élément triomphant des forces de la révolution socialiste. Nous avons en vue le caractère anticapitaliste, le caractère antipropriétaire de nos œuvres qui éduquent chez les lecteurs la volonté de lutte pour un avenir meilleur de l'humanité.

Whatever the general claims made by the Union or by Kirpotin, it soon becomes clear that socialist-realist writing is to be unashamedly didactic, aimed not simply at members of the working class hitherto cut off from literature but also at those middle-class readers who would be enlightened and instructed by it.

Although having initially been willing to follow the harder line prescribed by RAPP, *Commune* quickly adopted the cause of socialist realism. In the issue for May-June 1934 there appeared the first major statements about the new form of writing, an article by Yudin and Fadeev entitled 'Le Réalisme socialiste. Méthode fondamentale de la littérature soviétique'.

---

[1] For discussions of socialist realism in France and of the relationship between writers and intellectuals and the Communist Party, see in particular: J.-P. A. Bernard, *Le Parti communiste français et la question littéraire, 1921-1939* (Grenoble, 1972); D. Caute, *Communism and the French Intellectuals* (London, 1964); J.E. Flower, *Literature and the Left in France* (London, 1983). Much of what follows in this Introduction is based on these books in particular.

Like Kirpotin they claim that the essential quality of such
writing is that it is natural and not something imposed:

> Le réalisme socialiste n'est pas un dogme, un recueil de
> lois limitant la création artistique, réduisant toute la
> diversité des recherches et des formes à des
> commandements littéraires. Au contraire, le réalisme
> socialiste est l'expression naturelle des nouvelles relations
> socialistes et de la conception révolutionnaire du monde.[2]

Ideologically secure (rather than driven), it is claimed that
such writing will offer 'la peinture véridique et historiquement
concrète de la réalité dans son développement révolutionnaire'
and 'peut exposer la réalité dans son mouvement historique,
peut montrer comment l'avenir naît dans le présent'. Realistic
writing (or art) which simply depicts, however accurately, will
always be sterile, 'une photographie dépourvue d'importance
sociale et éducatrice'. In contrast, in a work of socialist-realist
inspiration, revolutionary socialism will be seen to penetrate
the very fabric of the work and will appear to be 'l'essence
même de l'œuvre, incarnée dans ses images'. The same claim
that somehow socialism would automatically be fundamental
to both content (*fond*) and style (*forme*) is also taken for
granted in a selection of the statutes and guidelines prepared
by the Union of Soviet Writers for a major congress to be held
in Moscow in August 1934. These were also published in
advance in *Commune* (May-June):

> Le réalisme socialiste assure à l'artiste une possibilité
> exceptionnelle de manifester son initiative créatrice, de
> choisir des genres, des formes et des méthodes variés. [...]
> Le but de l'Union des Écrivains Soviétiques est la création
> d'œuvres d'art dignes de la grande époque du socialisme.

With the benefit of hindsight it is easy to see how predictable
the themes of the major speeches at the Congress are.
Bourgeois literature was dismissed by Gorki for its decadence
and 'creative feebleness', and by Bukharin for its 'supernatural,

---

[2] See too the remark by Paul Vaillant-Couturier, in *Ceux qui ont choisi* (Paris,
1934): 'L'art et la littérature révolutionnaires et prolétariens ne doivent pas avoir pour
but l'exposé permanent et schématique d'une thèse. [...] Nous voulons combattre, nous ne
voulons pas bureaucratiser le combat' (p. 2).

mystic and otherworldly idealism'.[3] And even if Radek could recognize the value of the 'treasury of past literature' and acknowledge that proletarian writers could learn from it, he too saw salvation to lie only in socialism. The basic tone of the Congress was set in the opening address by Andrei Zhdanov, later to become Stalin's immensely influential Minister of Culture. Literature, he said, should combine 'truthfulness and historical concreteness [...] with the ideological remoulding and education of the toiling people in the spirit of socialism'; Radek again reminded congressists that henceforth literary realism should reflect the reality of socialism. Moreover, he said, 'socialist realism means not only knowing reality as it is, but knowing whither it is moving'. What is glaringly obvious from remarks such as these, and indeed from the proceedings of the Congress as a whole, is that content (ideological correctness), takes precedence over style, of which there is virtually no serious consideration at all. As Fadeev and Yudin had already claimed, there seemed to be general but unexplored conviction that a style of writing which would be both accessible and appropriate could somehow evolve naturally.

The official French representatives who contributed to the Moscow Congress were Aragon, Jean-Richard Bloch, Malraux and Vladimir Pozner. Nizan, who was already resident in the Soviet Union as editor of the French-language version of *International Literature*,[4] also attended but there is no record of his having contributed to any of the debates. The spirit in which the delegates went was summed up by the editorial of the August issue of *Commune*, which encouraged the establishment in France of 'la culture des Soviets' in order to revitalize the national cultural heritage. The following issue carried extracts from the speeches by Radek and Bukharin; in October, parts of Malraux's address, 'L'Art est une conquête' appeared; Bloch's intervention was reprinted in the September issue of *Europe*. Despite general sympathy and support, there were at the same time expressions of some caution. On 23 October, Malraux shared a platform with Gide at a public meeting in the Palais de la Mutualité in Paris. (Gide had not

---

[3] See H.G. Scott (ed.), *Soviet Writers' Congress 1934. The Debate on Socialist Realism and Modernism in the Soviet Union* (London, 1977).

[4] *International Literature* was published in Moscow in Russian, English, French and German between 1933 and 1939.

gone to Moscow,[5] but his current sympathy for the Communist party was well known.) They and Bloch could see through the apparently liberalising attitude of the Party to the prospect of another form of controlled writing. They also highlighted the Congress's failure to pay adequate attention to the literary qualities of socialist realism. Bloch warned against the constrictive dangers of the 'notions de masse', were they to be applied to literature. In an interview with Aragon, Malraux underlined the threat to a work of fiction if the novelist were to ignore individual psychological portrayal. Gide was even more direct: 'J'estime que toute littérature est en grand péril dès que l'écrivain se voit tenu d'obéir à un mot d'ordre' (*Commune*, November 1934).

In the middle of the following year, Bloch and Rolland returned to an even more specific aspect of the whole problem: language. In an article published in *Commune* in May, Rolland argued for the need to use a language in such literature which would be accessible to all potential readers. In the same issue Bloch was even more direct:

> Dans neuf cas sur dix, l'écrivain révolutionnaire doit encore sa formation aux humanités et à l'enseignement des lycées. Le problème qui se pose à lui est de rompre avec le système des complicités savantes, des métaphores entendues à demi mot et des allusions distinguées, sans verser pour cela dans une affectation dégoûtante de style 'peuple'.

Again with the benefit of hindsight on our part, this seems both obvious and important, but amongst those especially committed to socialist realism it seems all too frequently to have been ignored. Thus, for example, we find Nizan in his polemical pamphlet *Aden Arabie* or his second novel *Le Cheval de Troie* drawing much of his central imagery from the world of classical antiquity with which only his privileged bourgeois education would have allowed him to become familiar, even if he liked to deny such influence.

Apart from debates such as these, the only major statement directly concerning socialist realism as it might develop in France was Aragon's *Pour un réalisme socialiste*, a collection of five talks given between April and late June 1935. Fully

---

[5] Gide's *Retour de l'URSS* would be published by Gallimard in 1936.

committed to Communism, Aragon had an unshakeable faith in the inevitability of man's historical and social progress, what he termed 'la transformation du singe social de notre temps en l'homme socialiste de l'avenir'. Writers, he said, had a responsibility to illustrate within their works the benefits to be gained from socialism. But once again we find an emphasis on content rather than on form, on ideological direction rather than on the manner in which it is given literary expression. In virtually the only observation Aragon makes about style, he claims that a Soviet writer through his contacts with peasants and soldiers has created '[un] langage de l'avenir, compréhensible pour tous, sans abaissement de sa qualité technique'. Yet precisely how this has been achieved or what it is remain undisclosed and even, it seems, unconsidered.

By the late 1930s, this is where the elaboration of any theories about socialist realism remained for a decade or so. After the Liberation, and glowing from a reputation gained in the Resistance, the PCF enjoyed immense popularity and, until de Gaulle began in 1947 to remove Communist deputies from positions of ministerial responsibility, Communism was a real political force once again. In cultural matters this was equally the case, with influence coming directly from Moscow. Translations of Zhadnov's treatises on art, literature and music were widely disseminated and in France, Laurent Casanova and Jean Kanapa produced essays like *Le Communisme, la pensée et l'art* (1947), *Le Parti communiste, les intellectuels et la nation* (1949) or *Situation de l'intellectuel* (1957), in which the Soviet minister's blueprint was reformulated for national consumption. Heavily subsidised by the Party, 'official' publishing houses like the Éditions de la Nouvelle Critique, Les Éditions du PCF or Les Éditions Sociales produced novels which sold in tens of thousands. The annual 'Bataille du livre' at which Communist or sympathetic writers signed copies of their works attracted huge numbers and ensured a wide diffusion of both copies and ideas.

As de Gaulle's policy of exclusion took effect and the period of the Cold War began, however, what had had the appearance, and indeed appeal, of a fairly wide cultural campaign became increasingly narrow, dogmatic and Stalinist in tone. The review *La Nouvelle Critique* appeared in December 1948, and instantly became the vehicle for extreme orthodoxy. Zhdanovist directives became even more entrenched, and the socialist-realist writer emerged in a new and more militant guise: 'l'écrivain doit éduquer le peuple et l'armer idéologiquement'.[6] While some of the statements made in the 1930s may already have seemed prescriptive enough, in France at least they had relatively little direct effect on novel writing. Nearly twenty years later, adherence to Party cultural doctrine results in a series of works that are schematized, two-dimensional, transparently thin and naively didactic. Today we only have to read André Stil's trilogy *Le Premier Choc* (1952-1956), Pierre Courtade's *Jimmy* (1951) or Aragon's *Les Communistes* (1949-1951), for example, to see the extent to which the acceptance of such directives could lead some talented writers seemingly to close their eyes to the effect they would have on their work. Not all were quite so docile or unquestioning in their attitude, however, or at least were not so successful in preventing a critical dimension from expressing itself in their work, even indirectly. One such writer was Vailland whose lingering sympathy for certain elitist or individualist values did not fit easily with a Communist ethos. In each of his 'communist' novels, *Beau Masque* and *325 000 francs*, his study of power and sexual relationships and of broad social patterns allow him to escape from the stereotyping and narrow mould of socialist realism which some of his contemporaries accepted so willingly. And while there is no doubt about his depiction of a society in which capitalism dominates, in which workers are exploited, and from which escape is possible only through revolution, the overall picture to emerge is one in which the individual worker seems to be tragically trapped. Vailland, at this point in his career, was not opposed to the notion of the writer's responsibility or of the educative role to be played by the novel. Indeed, his essay *Expérience du drame*, while fundamentally about the theatre, is a unique and valuable contribution to the whole debate. As a novelist, though, Vailland retained his individuality simply because he was a better imaginative writer than Courtade, Stil or Aragon at this time. Malraux and Gide had been right. Talent could not—or certainly should not—prostitute itself. This was the itinerary on which Nizan had set out twenty years earlier. He sensed the danger and by the time he came to write *La Conspiration* was able to avoid it.

---

[6] A. Zhdanov, *Sur la littérature, la philosophie et la musique* (Paris, 1948), p. 36.

The making of a literary apparatchik

Nizan's passage through the maze of ideas surrounding left-wing, politically motivated literature during the 1930s is exemplary, and all the more so in that for him the two activities—politics and writing—were inseparable. This does not mean that he had a single, clearly formulated theory to enunciate, but through the dozens of articles which he contributed to such papers and reviews as *L'Humanité*, *Europe*, *Commune*, *Vendredi*, *La Revue des jeunes*, *Regards*, or *La Littérature internationale*, for example, a number of features regularly recur. Not surprisingly, Nizan is critical of modern capitalist, bourgeois society (though not without some ironic reflections on the benefits he had had from it himself) and of the kind of escapist literature—*évasion* and *divertissement* are words he uses frequently—which it fosters. But he is not content with being simply negatively critical. A parallel theme present in many of these articles and essays— and one which , as we have seen, was voiced by others—is that the writer has a responsibility to enlighten and to educate; like the political journalist, he has a duty to engage his readers in a form of dialogue or pact from which they will emerge persuaded of the need to see beyond the present and, guided by the revolutionary socialist values which have been explained to them, will move towards a better future. In a major article, 'Une littérature responsable' (*Vendredi*, 8 November 1935) Nizan wrote:

> Il ne faut pas enseigner le désespoir mais, au-delà du tableau intolérable de notre monde, dégager les valeurs impliquées par l'action de la colère des hommes qui veulent bouleverser leur sort. Cette littérature jouerait plus sur l'avenir que sur le présent, sur des volontés que sur des constatations, elle dirait moins aux hommes ce qu'ils sont que ce qu'ils veulent confusément être. Un rapport de responsabilité l'unirait à ses lecteurs; elle s'occuperait plutôt d'accroître leur conscience d'eux-mêmes que de leur procurer des plaisirs.

By 1935 and the time he came to write these words, Nizan was one of the PCF's major and most influential intellectuals. His apprenticeship, to the point when, in James Steel's phrase, he could be considered to correspond 'presque parfaitement au portrait robot du révolutionnaire professionnel',[7] had been rapid, if not entirely classic. Left-wing sympathies and subversive activities had marked his years at the École normale supérieure; he had flirted briefly with the extreme right-wing ideas of Georges Valois and his neo-fascist group the Faisceau. By 1926 he was involved with the radical review *Philosophies* and its sequel *L'Esprit* which he described as being characterized by 'la mystique bolcheviste' and, despite being tempted to embark on a business career, he joined the Communist Party towards the end of 1927. Described by Simone de Beauvoir in *La Force de l'âge* as being at this time 'un révolté plutôt qu'un révolutionnaire',[8] he soon began to acquire the discipline to adjust and serve the Party well in the next few years. By 1929 he was a member of the militant group around *La Revue marxiste* part of whose intention, stated in its first editorial (1 February 1929), would remain as a constant value for him:

> *La Revue marxiste* veut devenir l'organe de tous les travailleurs qui cherchent à développer leurs connaissances du marxisme et du féminisme, ainsi que des intellectuels désireux de se placer sur le terrain du prolétariat et de sa conception matérialiste et décidés à ne plus se laisser endormir par la pensée mystique et idéaliste.

Within two years Nizan was given his first tasks as a Party intellectual. These involved taking disciplinary measures against the reviews *Bifur* and *Monde* which were seen to be deviating from Party directives at a time when ideological orthodoxy was becoming increasingly stringent. For the former, he was already well placed. Having failed to find a position with Gallimard, Nizan became the 'directeur littéraire' of the publishers Carrefour, whose owner, Pierre Lévy, also produced *Bifur*. Through Nizan's influence it was hoped that the periodical, while not becoming 'officiellement communiste', would be 'entièrement sous notre direction'. In its

---

[7] J. Steel, 'Paul Nizan: l'apprentissage d'un apparatchik ou les conséquences du refus (1927-1934)', in B. Alluin & J. Deguy (eds.), *Paul Nizan écrivain* (Lille, 1988), p. 35.

[8] *La Force de l'âge* (Paris, 1960), p. 491.

'new' form, *Bifur* had one further issue only, and Nizan was generally held to have been responsible for its collapse. His second target, Barbusse's *Monde*, had been heavily criticized at the Kharkov conference for alleged liberal tendencies. Nizan's plan was to replace a number of the editorial board by more militant Party members, including himself as literary editor. As he wrote to Barbusse on 11 March 1931, this would help 'réaliser un travail véritablement utile et fécond'; moreover with such a change 'les déviations et les confusions disparaîtront rapidement avec ceux-là même qui avaient intérêt à les maintenir'.[9] As an elder statesman of the Left and one who had been more responsible than most for the diffusion of cultural and ideological news from the Soviet Union during the previous decade, Barbusse did not take kindly to such interference and proposals. In a letter of some dignity but in which his irritation was clear, he replied that such action would 'transformer *Monde* en un journal communiste 100%, c'est-à-dire [...] jeter à bas toute l'initiative tactique qui [...] constituait et constitue la raison d'être du journal'. Furthermore he accused Nizan and his colleagues of being 'animés par un sectarisme juvénile', an irritation which Nizan would have resurface as part of an ironic *autocritique* in *La Conspiration* seven years later. Largely because he was responsible for financing the production of *Monde* Barbusse had his way and the review would be published for another four years. Nizan's attacks nonetheless continued. In an article 'La Littérature révolutionnaire en France' (*La Revue des vivants*, September 1932), he wrote:

> Le groupe *Monde*, c'est le groupe des traîtres. [...] *Monde* est devenu un papier social démocrate et radical socialiste qui joue un rôle de confusion dangereux, qui répandit dans les couches de lecteurs ouvriers un brouillard propre à toutes les conspirations bourgeoises.

None of this, however, prevented Nizan from contributing to *Monde* himself. In the very month, March 1931, when he was acting as Party disciplinarian, he published 'Secrets de famille', a long attack on bourgeois society and values in which

---

[9] This exchange is reproduced in A. Cohen-Solal and H. Nizan, *Paul Nizan, communiste impossible* (Paris, 1980). The original letters are in the Nizan archive at the IMEC (see below, note 14).

he tried, somewhat absurdly, to prove that despite his recent past, within a generation he was a true member of the working class. Whether the publication of the article was a coincidence or piece of opportunism on Nizan's part is impossible to say, but by now he was certainly voicing—at least officially—the hard, proletarian line peddled at Kharkov.

With articles such as this, and with the publication of his essays *Aden Arabie* (1931) and *Les Chiens de garde* (1932), Nizan's status within the vanguard of the PCF's intellectuals was secure. But like all apparatchiks he would soon modify his position as Party policy assumed its new, more open and conciliatory direction. When *Commune* was first published, Nizan, together with Aragon, was given secretarial responsibilities and in 1934 he was invited to go to Moscow, where, as we have noted, he was responsible for *La Littérature internationale*. Having attended the Writers' Congress in August 1934 he was soon proclaiming the virtues of socialist realism with just as much conviction as he had those of revolutionary proletarian writing only three years earlier. Once again, however, a careful reading of his articles reveals the same concern that the writer's responsibility should be to expose and to enlighten. Thus in his review of Aragon's *Pour un réalisme socialiste* in *L'Humanité* (12 August 1935), he praises his fellow Communist for having underlined socialist realism's 'capacité de perspectives', for the manner in which it goes beyond traditional bourgeois realism, 'un reálisme-critique [qui] décrivait amèrement la réalité [mais qui] ne voyait point d'issue à cette réalité'. What is essential, Nizan claims, is the future:

> Un réalisme socialiste met au premier plan cet avenir qu'il contribue à faire naître, avec une certaine exaltation. Ce qui ne signifie pas que cette importance donnée à l'avenir de la réalité soit optimiste et comporte la facilité. Ce qui s'oppose au pessimisme bourgeois, c'est beaucoup moins un optimisme satisfait qu'un héroïsme tragique qui voit le mal qu'ont les hommes à transformer la réalité.

The same point is also made in a review of Tristan Rémy's *Les Grandes Lignes* in July 1937: 'Chaque parole importante des personnages comporte la référence à l'avenir que comporte tout climat épique. Le lien de la réalité et de l'avenir qu'elle

exige est sans doute le secret du réalisme socialiste'
(*L'Humanité*, 7 July 1937). But as in the case of Aragon, and
indeed others who were proclaiming the virtues of this new
writing, it is difficult to ascertain whether Nizan paid any
attention at all to its formal or stylistic qualities; as for so
many, it is the political direction or weight of the text which
come first. A small hint that he may have been aware of this
problem is apparent from a negative review of Mauriac's *Les
Anges noirs* published in *L'Humanité*, 22 March 1936.
'Mauriac', Nizan wrote, 'est catholique et sa religion domine
son art. Il y a un combat entre le croyant et le romancier où le
romancier est toujours vaincu.' (For 'Catholic', substitute
'Communist'.) More positively, in a tribute to Eugène Dabit in
September of the same year (*L'Humanité*, 6 September 1936),
he suggested that the task of the socialist-realist writer was to
'faire passer la révolte dans l'art, sans détruire l'art'.
Fortunately Nizan was never guilty of producing the kind of
simplistic statement made some twenty years later by André
Stil, who in *Vers le réalisme socialiste* (1952) remarked: 'La
politique, dans le roman, devient le sucre dans l'eau. Si le sucre
n'est pas bien fondu, quand on vous offre un verre d'eau
sucrée, c'est qu'il n'est pas bien préparé.' At the same time,
precisely how the appropriate balance of content and form
should be achieved, or even what Nizan understood by it, was
not addressed by him here or elsewhere any more than it was
by anyone else.

What does remain constant in his attitude, however, is the
insistance on the communicative link between writer and
reader. In a review of André Philippe's novel *L'Acier*
(*L'Humanité*, 7 August 1937), the first winner of the Prix
Ciment, he praised the author for having succeeded in
establishing 'le rapport [...] au peuple, auquel il se sent uni'. And
in his last major statement about the novel, 'Ambition du
roman moderne' (*Cahiers de la jeunesse*, April 1939) he would
return once again to this and to those other qualities which, for
him, were the hallmarks of the new and only valid form of
writing. The article finishes with a flourish and the tone of a
manifesto:

> Ce qui me semble essentiel pour le lecteur comme pour le
> romancier qui forment un couple—et un couple, cela fait
> toujours deux complices—c'est de diriger la complicité

dans le sens le plus exigeant. La vraie fonction du lecteur,
c'est de vouloir apprendre à vivre, par conséquent de
considérer le roman, la littérature en géneral, non pas du
tout comme un divertissement à la fois vulgaire et
pascalien du mot, mais comme un instrument de
connaissance.

Ceci vous donnera l'ambition complémentaire du
romancier de considérer le roman avant tout comme un
instrument de connaissance et non comme un
instrument de diversion.

Tout me semble résumé dans une formule saisissante de
Marx: Marx s'interrogeant sur les fonctions de la
philosophie—il ne parlait pas de mission—se résumait
ainsi: il faut donner aux gens la conscience d'eux-mêmes.
Et il ajoute cette petite proposition qui me paraît décisive
et sur laquelle je veux terminer: même s'ils ne le veulent
pas.

What is also new in this article is Nizan's claim that not only
should the novel deal with reality (as distinct from *évasion*) but
that such reality should be contemporaneous with the
novelist's experience and with the act of writing. In other
words the novelist should formulate an immediate response to
that reality and interpret it for the benefit of his reader. The
idea that there should be a time-lag before an event can
become the legitimate subject of a novel is 'une difficulté
inventée par des critiques frivoles'. Perhaps with an unspoken
allusion to novels like Aragon's *Les Cloches de Bâle* or *Les
Beaux Quartiers,* which draw on the early years of the century
for a good deal of their subject matter and in which the author
blurs chronology for novelistic effect, Nizan allows some
latitude ('pour eux, l'actualité commence en 1918'), but his clear
preference is for 'l'actualité [qui] commence à un moment qui
correspond au début de son expérience la plus intense'.
    This clearly is something Nizan had practised himself in his
first two novels, *Antoine Bloyé* (1933) and *Le Cheval de Troie*
(1935). In the former, very largely a fictionalised account of his
own father's life, he confronts the critical issue faced by so
many intellectuals at that time: that of class allegiance and
betrayal. This, we should recall, was also fundamental to
'Secrets de famille', his *Monde* article of the same year. The
novel opens with the discovery by Pierre Bloyé of his father's

corpse. Thereafter he returns to his father's birth to recount and reconstruct Antoine's life. Since this is now over and closed, the account can only be read as a kind of warning or lesson for the son, and for the reader. What we are given is the description of the life and career of a man, constrained and even determined by certain factors but who, by virtue of his intelligence and capacity for hard work, gradually improves himself economically and socially. Antoine rises from being a railway employee to a member of the management, but in so doing becomes increasingly isolated. In order to underscore the sociopolitical point he is making Nizan shows Bloyé at moments to be aware that he has betrayed his class yet unable to settle in his 'new' one. When it was published, *Antoine Bloyé* was hailed, especially by Aragon as an example of socialist realism, but for Susan Suleiman, it is so only in a negative sense.[10] There is no exemplary or educative dimension to Antoine's experience pointing the way forward to others towards a new and better future. Despite the occasional nostalgic memory of his humble origins, Bloyé remains passive, sometimes ignorant ('il ne savait pas que ...' is one of Nizan's recurring narrative ploys) and a victim of pressures brought to bear on him by the social class to which he eventually accedes but which will discard him, leaving him to die. The indictment of the bourgeoisie in this first novel is clear, therefore, but suggestions as to how it might be positively overthrown are at best only implied. This is an example of the kind of critical realism which Nizan found limited and wanted to go beyond. This he did two years later with *Le Cheval de Troie*.

As the title of this novel indicates, we have a story of subterfuge and subversion from within, which may, of course, be read as a metaphor for Marx's theory that capitalism carries within itself the seeds of its own destruction. With memories of the confrontation between Fascists and Communists in Paris in February 1934 still fresh (Nizan's preference for the 'actual'), the novel charts the organized resistance by the Left to a fascist rally in Villefranche. The result is a bloody street battle which leaves the workers victorious but at a cost, and there is no suggestion that their success is any more than a single stage in a long, epic struggle

---

10 'Pour une poétique du roman à thèse: l'exemple de Nizan', *Critique*, 330 (November 1974), 995-1021.

'to change the world'. But while limited in this way the immediate message of *Le Cheval de Troie* is positive. Once again as in *Antoine Bloyé* the values of bourgeois society are shown to be shallow, oppressive and based on self-interest, but in this novel they are challenged and overthrown, albeit temporarily.

It is true that after his first novel, *Le Cheval de Troie* shows a marked shift towards optimism, but it is unashamedly didactic and all too frequently runs the risk of schematization. The debate is often presented in simplistic, oppositional terms and there are incidents whose symbolic value outweighs any intrinsic human, psychological interests they might otherwise have had—Paul's martyrdom or the loss of Catherine's baby for example. The same contrast is found in aspects of the novel's style as well. The eerie, subaquatic imagery which is characteristic of the fascist meetings or of certain oppressive institutions (notably the church) elementally at odds with that of fire and the warmth of comradeship of the Left. The fascist presence fades into the night. Bloyé and Marie-Louise watch the sun rise on a new dawn from the east. Many passages in the novel are written in slogan form, full of conviction, and Nizan never hesitates to allow his omniscient authorial voice to cut across his text to interpret, inform or even anticipate. Certainly there are other features which lend the novel a darker, sinister and more interesting human dimension— perhaps the political equivalent of Gide's Devil. Thus in particular the schoolteacher Lange, who lives in a kind of twilight world, is cynical, sexually confused and sympathizes with the forces of order and fascism. Like Pluvinage in *La Conspiration*, whom he foreshadows, he is a failure, and can only try to prove himself through revenge. Even more marked is the novel's obsession with death. Already fundamental to *Antoine Bloyé*, death in *Le Cheval de Troie* finds its fullest expression as a political and philosophical concern in Nizan's work. Jacqueline Leiner[11] has seen this obsession to be even more significant as an inspirational force than Marxism, and it is a well-known fact that barely a day passed for Nizan without his referring to it. In an immediate sociopolitical context in *Le Cheval de Troie*—and indeed in *La Conspiration*

---

[11] J. Leiner, *Le Destin littéraire de Paul Nizan et ses étapes successives* (Paris, 1970), pp. 182-5.

as well— death represents passivity and a surrender to the oppressive forces of capitalism and of bourgeois society. (In this we have a strong reminder of Kyo's remark in Malraux's *La Condition humaine*: 'mourir est passivité'.) Death therefore has to be resisted, and may even be converted into a motivating force. In this second novel, for example, Catherine dies as a result not only of her own ignorance or carelessness, but also because society has failed to provide her with the necessary instruction and support. But at the same time her death launches her husband, Albert, into commitment and positive action. A similar statement appears to be made in *La Conspiration*, when, at the end, Laforgue nearly dies but recovers to be 'reborn'. Yet it is doubtful whether this is unambiguously a positive sign. In Nizan's last novel, particularly in view of the retrospective nature of the narration, death (real or metaphorical) remains vital to his perception of life and of the sociopolitical forces which shape it.

La Conspiration

A question of perspective

Le Cheval de Troie was written at the peak of Nizan's political orthodoxy and at a time when, as we have seen, socialist realism was being most widely acclaimed and practised. Also, in terms of its content the novel conforms almost perfectly to the criteria Nizan would outline for the modern novel in his article for the *Cahiers de la Jeunesse* four years later. Between these two dates there is nothing in Nizan's published work, nor indeed anything in the way of private writing (letters, diaries, etc.), to suggest that he remained, to use Michael Scriven's phrase, any less than 'resolutely communist'.[12] It seems reasonable therefore to suppose that the criteria or formulae for any novel he would write would remain the same. When, then, the anonymous presentation of the novel in the Folio edition of *La Conspiration* defines it as 'un des rares romans français «réalistes-socialistes» intelligents, qui ne sacrifie jamais la forme, le style, l'humour, la poésie au fond ou à la volonté de prouver' (an obvious allusion to Gide's words of warning mentioned above, pp. 6; 8), it might appear that Nizan had arrived at some form of perfection. But the claim is misleading. While there are undoubtedly features of *La Conspiration* which situate it within or link it to the tradition of socialist realism, it is too complex and ultimately too ambiguous to allow such a neat, all-embracing definition.

Like his two earlier novels, *La Conspiration* depends, at least indirectly, on a number of autobiographical elements. His own years at the École normale supérieure (1924-1926) provide the context for his group of young protagonists; *La Guerre civile* was the title of a projected review which, it was hoped, would bridge the gap between the relatively moderate views of Barbusse's *Clarté*, the iconoclastic, anti-bourgeois tirades of

---

12 M. Scriven, *Paul Nizan: Communist Novelist* (Basingstoke, 1988), p. 158.

the Surrealists and the *Philosophies* group. As Marcel Fourrier, a contributor to *Clarté* but someone strongly opposed to Barbusse's control, remarked, *La Guerre civile* would be 'le premier courant qui apparaît en France depuis 1919 d'une jeune intelligence révolutionnaire acquise au communisme.'[13] It was never published. It is also generally agreed that for *La Guerre civile* of the novel, Nizan drew on *La Revue marxiste*, which in turn fell victim to Stalin's need to control (or his fear of) Party intellectuals. Nizan's acute attack of appendicitis in December 1927 and his near death are accepted by most critics as providing the model for Laforgue's illness. Laforgue, like Nizan (we should remember 'Secrets de famille'), prefers to think of his true roots being those of peasant stock; his father too is an engineer. The descriptions of Simon's military life are probably based on Nizan's own military service. And so on.

The incorporation of such details in *La Conspiration* is, in itself, not particularly significant, but the manner in which Nizan focuses on a period (1928-1929) which predates that of the novel's composition by almost a decade, and moreover displaces the events on which that period is based (1924-1926) by four years, calls for attention. It might be argued, of course, that such a slippage is insignificant and that a period of ten— or even fourteen—years is safely within the time-frame, the *actualité*, which Nizan allows in his discussion of the novel in 'L'Ambition du roman moderne'. But within pages it becomes apparent that the gap creates an important perspective. The narrator is removed from the earlier time slot, allowing a degree of interplay between the two periods and thereby retrospective comment and even judgement. There is a further, more detailed but no less significant point, too. In the first version of *La Conspiration*, Bloyé is called Levêque.[14] By renaming him, Nizan restores a link with *Antoine Bloyé* and *Le Cheval de Troie*, and in a sense invites his readers to see the three novels as a block. But in terms of the chronology of the action of the novels, the Bloyé of *La Conspiration predates* the one of *Le Cheval de Troie*. In the last novel he is a marginal

---

[13] 'De Clarté à La Guerre civile', *Clarté*, 79 (December 1925-January 1926), quoted in J. Steel, *Paul Nizan: un révolutionnaire conformiste?* (Paris, 1987), p. 50.

[14] The Nizan archive is held by the Institut Mémoires de l'Édition Contemporaine (IMEC), where it may be consulted. There is a complete typescript of the novel and another of most of it, both slightly corrected by Nizan, but no complete manuscript.

character only, or, to quote James Steel, the 'esquisse d'un révolutionnaire [...] sans relief et figé'. For Adèle King he is an 'observateur des folies des autres',[15] and he has several years to go before he will become the militant activist we have already seen in the second novel. If, in turn, we then consider the chronology of the novel's composition, a different perspective emerges. Nizan 'knows' in 1938 what he would have—has already had—Bloyé become in 1935, and yet at the close of *La Conspiration* he has Laforgue reflect:

> Philippe s'imaginait qu'ils se reverraient dix ans plus tard, les années de professorat en province achevées, avec des femmes et des enfants qui se regardaient de travers, et n'ayant pour ne pas se taire ensemble que des souvenirs refroidis d'École Normale et de Sorbonne.
> «Nous n'irons pas très loin», pensa-t-il. (301)

Such a comment is, as we shall see, a fitting reflection on the issues which Nizan explores in his last novel; it is entirely in keeping with the prevailing tone of caution and uncertainty. It may well be that in 1937-1938 Nizan has 'forgotten' the evolution he has already had Bloyé undergo. But when we consider the dates of both plot and composition of *La Conspiration*, it is difficult not to be of the opinion that even if he is not offering an open critique of the previous decade, Nizan is reflecting ironically, and moreover pessimistically, on the possibility of effective political or revolutionary activity. And on his own role during it.

A world of jellyfish[16]

Before we look more closely at this dimension of the novel and the way Nizan deals with it in terms of both content and form, we should remind ourselves of what *La Conspiration* is about and how, from a first reading, the irony of the title begins to show. The *first* conspiracy is self-evident. Headed by Bernard Rosenthal a group of five young intellectuals plan to

---

[15] J. Steel, *op. cit.*, pp. 139-40; A. King, *Paul Nizan, écrivain* (Paris, 1976), p. 136.

[16] See the 'amas sans queue ni tête de gélatine, [...] espèce de grande méduse avec des organes bien cachés' (30) quotation below (p. 22).

launch a review, *La Guerre civile*, in which they intend to publish subversive and compromising material. Initially the review enjoys some success ('cinq cents abonnés et huit cents acheteurs au numéro'[65]), but the only two subjects about which we learn anything are first, the details of military action to be taken in the event of a popular uprising in Paris, and second, the plans of a new industrial heating system. Neither will be published, and when Laforgue discovers the relevant papers among Rosenthal's effects after his death they are 'jaunis comme si Rosenthal était mort depuis dix ans'(242). In view of what we have already noted about the dates of publication and of the plot of *La Conspiration*, this period of a decade is not without interest, and the insignificance of these two subjects in terms of their contribution to potential revolutionary activity is obvious. But in any case the project is subverted within months of its having been launched as *other* conspiracies come into play. Rosenthal falls in love with his sister-in-law and their brief but intense affair is, at least for him, a direct challenge to the bourgeois morality and values of his family. But it too will be short-lived, as the family, on the discovery of the affair, closes in and reasserts itself. Of the other four conspirators, Bloyé, as we have already noted, plays virtually no part in the plot, and Jurien (is there an ironic play on *jurer* and *rien*?) is even less in evidence. There remain Pluvinage, in many respects a kind of mirror image of Rosenthal, who is powerless to resist the hereditary influences which lead him to become a police informer, and Laforgue, who has a vital role throughout as a voice of criticism, especially of Rosenthal, and one also of caution and reason. (In this he is often cast in the role of an 'alternative' to the omniscient author.)

At the end of the novel Laforgue falls seriously ill, and while his recovery is described literally as a rebirth, there is a threat that he too could be reabsorbed by his family, however much he may try to resist. What begins, therefore, as an attempt by these young men to subvert all that is represented by the capitalist bourgeois society to which they belong is turned completely on its head as that same society, and indeed life in general, conspire to defeat them as they defeat all dissidents. However pessimistic may appear Laforgue's assessment of his fellow conspirators as he imagines they will be in 1938-1939 (**301**), it is surely significant. But it is not only through his description of the events, of the characters individually, and of the relationships between them, that Nizan conveys this impression. Though it is less obvious than in *Le Cheval de Troie*, from the very beginning of the novel he allows his omniscient authorial voice to comment and to interpret, and in so doing he establishes the kind of dialogue with the reader which he considered so essential. This procedure also reveals the elements if not of personal disillusion, then certainly of an *autocritique* which is sustained throughout and is a, if not the, major contributory factor to the novel's ultimate ambiguity.

None of this is to suggest that Nizan has no sympathy or tolerance for his young protagonists, but with the benefit of hindsight, wisdom and more importantly the judgement which it permits, are rarely absent. Already we read in Chapter I:

> On ne peut pas dire qu'ils soient absolument dupes de leurs discours sur la métamorphose du monde [...] ils se sentent révolutionnaires, ils pensent que la seule noblesse réside dans la volonté de subversion. C'est entre eux un dénominateur commun, bien qu'ils soient sans doute destinés à devenir des étrangers ou des ennemis. (30)

Their youth excuses them a great deal:

> ... comme ils ignorent tout de la vie que mènent les hommes entre leur travail et leur femme, leurs patrons et leurs enfants, leurs petites manies et leurs grands malheurs, il n'y a encore au fond de leur politique que des métaphores et des cris... (30)

Their aims and their 'volonté de subversion' are to be admired (and had they not, in Nizan's own case, flourished in his early essays?), but they are not yet in a position to know the strength or the resistance of the society and its institutions which they hope to destabilise. The warning narrator's voice makes this very point on the same page and with an image which recalls (or anticipates...) the viscous, subaquatic ones of *Le Cheval de Troie*:

> Ils ne savaient pas encore comme c'est lourd et mou le monde, comme il ressemble peu à un mur qu'on flanque par terre pour en monter un autre beaucoup plus beau, mais à un amas sans queue ni tête de gélatine, à une espèce de grande méduse avec des organes bien cachés. (30)

And if this were not enough, Nizan also by the same methods underlines the difficulty, even impossibility, of translating ideological conviction into effective action. Once more the time-lag between plot and composition may be relevant. In *L'Humanité* (10 February 1931), an anonymous reviewer of *Aden Arabie* wrote: 'le marxisme n'est pas seulement une théorie du socialisme, c'est aussi et surtout une nécessité de l'action révolutionnaire. Un intellectuel marxiste n'est marxiste que dans la mesure où il est militant.' From the early planning stages of *La Guerre civile*, Nizan makes no secret of his young conspirators' immaturity:

> Ils se laissaient d'ailleurs aller jusqu'à croire avec une complaisance excessive que la Révolution était faite au moment où ils ne se sentaient décidément plus solidaires de la bourgeoisie, et une sorte d'orgueil satisfait les faisait parler de la conscience post-révolutionnaire; personne n'aurait songé à les trouver dangereux.(60)

Whatever Rosenthal may claim as his ambitions for the review, we are also told that its articles 'n'avaient pas de chances sérieuses d'ébranler le capitalisme'(64). To be fair, he does recognize this, writing to Laforgue: 'La Révolution exige de nous des actes qui soient aussi efficaces que ceux du chrétien, aussi éloignés de la vie intérieure, et qui nous compromettent assez pour que nous ne puissions jamais *retourner*'(81), whereas their articles and speeches will not achieve this in the short term. As a consequence he has Simon steal the military documents, but does so at absolutely no risk to himself. Nor is this 'act' likely to have much, if any, practical effect. Régnier and Laforgue are quick to point this out, and the latter, so often the voice of reason in the novel, echoes the caution expressed by *L'Humanité*'s reviewer, and carries Nizan's *own* critical reflections forward into the rest of the novel:

> ... ton idée dostoïevskienne [...] me paraît incroyablement romantique. S'il est question d'engagement, j'ai comme une impression que l'engagement d'un metallurgiste dans une cellule du parti, dans une cellule d'usine, va beaucoup plus loin que n'importe quelle manifestation à la fois retorse et mystique. [...] Tes songes clandestins me paraissent [...] plus efficaces en vue de ta perfection personnelle que pour la réussite concrète de la conquête du pouvoir politique par le prolétariat.(85-6)

From very early on, therefore, there is a sense, induced by various factors and underlined by Nizan's own hindsight expressed through his narratorial commentary, that the ambitions of these young men will inevitably founder. Indeed it seems more than a simple coincidence—or more than an element in Nizan's topographical accuracy—that as early as the third paragraph of the novel there should be a specific reference to the rue Claude-Bernard, named after the founder of the theory of physiological and hereditary determinism.[17] Equally significant seems to be the fact that at the end of his *récit* Pluvinage should blame what he defines as 'une affreuse fatalité'(300) for the way his life has evolved. In fact these two allusions to fate and inevitability are like parentheses around the main part of the book. Beyond them, in the final chapter, Laforgue may be offered a possible glimmer of hope, but it is not assured.

The society against which Rosenthal and his friends like to think they are in revolt is claustrophobic and middle-class. There are no representatives of the working class in this novel, merely a passing allusion to them in the description of the 'petit monde clos'(23) in the opening pages. Here, Nizan's authorial voice distinguishes between the middle-class women discarding the garments which are so emblematic of their society and their servants, occasionally heard but not seen:

> C'étaient [...] des dames entre deux âges qui enlevaient des corsets, des ceintures et des gaines comme des pièces d'armure; les plus jeunes habitantes de ces maisons, celles dont les chansons jaillissaient parfois du fond d'une cuisine, couchaient sous les combles: on ne les voyait pas.(12)

And this passage closes with an image that recalls those that were so indicative of enforced conformity in *Le Cheval de Troie*. As the bustle and life of the area fall silent, 'il y avait [...] des moments où une espèce de grand silence marin déferlait paresseusement sur les récifs de la ville'(12).

---

[17] The street name may not be randomly chosen, if it is intended to suggest the struggle between Rosenthal and his older brother, which the latter, as family representative, will win. In the invention of a fictional cul-de-sac leading off this street, the *impasse* Claude-Bernard, Gide takes a dig at scientism (*Les Caves du Vatican*). Could the name Rosenthal be satirical (see below, p. 34, n. 18)? We recall that Gide's *Les Faux-Monnayeurs* has another Bernard... Profitendieu!

Silence and conformity, what Nizan elsewhere calls 'le ronronnement perpétuel' (70), are soon perceived to be the hallmarks of this society. In *La Conspiration*, as indeed throughout his work, capitalist society is made up of structured blocks or units, each with its own rules and rituals which are imposed on individuals or are used to seduce them so that they remain acquiescent or can be controlled. This is a classic Marxist view. In such a world people are no more than objects, to be bought or sold at will. Catherine, for example, is described by Bernard as 'un bien meuble que sa famille avait acquis au cours d'une vente solennelle'(153). Significantly, for all his scorn, his own attitude is barely different: 'Nous partirons, j'ai un peu d'argent, nous ne serons même pas pauvres'(191). In this respect, of course, *La Conspiration* is no different from either of Nizan's previous works. In *Antoine Bloyé* it is the world of business and management which shapes people's lives; in *Le Cheval de Troie* it is education, the Church and the forces of order; in *La Conspiration* it is above all the family and social connections: 'les pouvoirs publics et les familles conspiraient comme autrefois à les faire retomber dans de brillants avenirs, des carrières, des soucis d'avancement, d'argent, de beaux mariages.' (68-9)

A self-contained example can be found in the neat cameo of army life in Chapters VIII and IX. Simon owes his position to Pauline's contacts and when, having been discovered copying the secret documents, he claims to be using the material for a novel, he is immediately treated with leniency: 'ils n'auraient peut-être pas cru un fils d'ouvrier sur parole, mais Simon les trompa avec une grande aisance'(116-7).

Fundamental to this society and what cements it together is an unquestioning and willing acceptance of habit. There is a recipe that is universally adaptable: repetition and familiarity ensure protection for those within and at the same time create the impression of unity and stability to those outside. The Rosenthals are typical: 'c'était une famille qui se plaisait, comme toutes les autres, à composer des images rassurantes de sa cohésion et de sa permanence'(154). They transport their lifestyle around with them. Thus, despite clichéd remarks about the beauty and silence of the Normandy countryside, in summer they do their best to recreate 'les divertissements sociaux de l'hiver à Paris. Les semaines de vacances s'y passaient en conversations, en correspondances continuelles de domaine à domaine, en visites, en cérémonies urbaines qu'on nommait relations de voisinage'(162-3). This is a society of philistine *nouveaux riches*, a complete change from a time two generations earlier when art and culture were still recognized as having some value and when money was not an end in itself, but 'la condition temporelle d'une vie consacrée à des soucis nobles, à la connaissance du monde'(169). But if this is what has been imposed by a new metropolitan and essentially Parisian caste, those who have remained buried in their provincial properties have little more to offer that is better, having become ultra-conservative, tyrannical and even inbred. Much of Nizan's description of these life-styles is ironic and caricatural, of course, but it is also deeply serious. In addition to creating a façade for others and a protective carapace for themselves (we should not forget 'des corsets, des ceintures et des gaines comme des pièces d'armure'[12]), such lifestyles also create an illusion of immortality: 'tout semblait protéger les Rosenthal des malheurs, de la peur, de la mort'(154). And yet already their lives are a form of death. Although references to it are less frequent than in *Le Cheval de Troie*, death is just as dominant and significant in *La Conspiration*. When Laforgue remarks, 'Il faudrait être absolument délivré de la peur de mourir'(13), he is voicing the key to Nizan's personal and political philosophy. But again chronology, both of plot and composition, is important. While the commitment of Albert, the martyrdom of Paul and the end of *Le Cheval de Troie* suggest optimism in 1935, the ultimate message in 1938 seems distinctly less assured.

Although there are occasional references to the families of Bloyé, Julien and Laforgue, Nizan's attack on bourgeois capitalist society is directed in particular at the Rosenthal family. Édouard Rosenthal and his older son Claude are both brokers. Even if the latter has embraced modern economic theories, much to his father's disgust, continuity between them is assured. Thus, in keeping with the values of their society, Édouard Rosenthal does not see death as a threat, since stability and reinforcement of those values are guaranteed. Nizan comments omnisciently:

> Il voyageait peu. Il ambitionnait de devenir syndic de la Compagnie, d'être promu commandeur de la Légion d'Honneur. Ensuite il mourrait: la mort ne lui semblait

> pas absolument effrayante, il n'avait pas ce qu'il faut
> d'imagination pour se révolter devant les paradoxes du
> néant, il souhaitait seulement souffrir peu, s'éteindre ou
> mourir d'une embolie, d'une rupture d'anévrisme, en
> dormant. (135-6)

The Rosenthals' world is a closed, unproductive one and
Nizan's descriptions of it contain overt references to
cemeteries or monumental tombs. When Bernard returns to the
family home in the heart of the bourgeois enclave that is the
sixteenth *arrondissement*, it is to 'La Muette, où les gens vivent
dans de trop grands coquillages de pierre, le long des rues
nettes comme des allées de cimetières à concessions
perpétuelles'(16). The description of the family house carries
this further, with suggestions, too, of a hospital or clinic which
anticipate the link to be made between Rosenthal and
Pluvinage:

> On suivait d'abord un grand couloir de pierre blanche
> coupée par de longues glaces et de sanglantes banquettes
> de velours grenat et on arrivait au rez-de-chaussée des
> Rosenthal. C'était un grand appartement qui donnait par
> des portes-fenêtres sur un jardin humide entouré de
> grilles et obscurci par les hauts immeubles blancs.(21)

This is the protective world from which Bernard claims he
will escape, but from the beginning the signs are there that its
hold on him is too strong. When, for example, he argues that he
needs to be nearer to the rue d'Ulm in order to avoid
unnecessary journeys across Paris (though in reality in the hope
of setting up home with Catherine), the flat is entirely
redecorated at his father's expense and the rent paid for him
(199). Bernard is like Catherine Simonidzé, in Aragon's *Les
Cloches de Bâle*, who relies on a monthly allowance from her
wealthy Georgian father so that she can afford to be treated
for tuberculosis in a private Swiss sanatorium. Catherine
evolves from a position of personal independence through
anarchy to socialism under the guidance of Victor, but she
never completely cuts free from her background and privileges
to become politically active. Nor will Bernard. Already Nizan's
description of the pictures in his room suggests this, each one
being an unambiguous signal of the different values and their
impact on his life: 'une mauvaise lithographie de Lénine, une

assez bonne reproduction du Descartes de Hals et un petit paysage métaphysique de Chirico'(**22**). Equally indicative is his behaviour when he returns to his room after the meeting when the decision to set up *La Guerre civile* is taken: 'Bernard prit un bain et se coucha, pensant qu'il avait décidément trop fumé et qu'il avait un peu faim; il songea ensuite vaguement à la Révolution, et précisément à sa famille [...] il avait vraiment sommeil, il s'endormit enfin'(**22-3**). However angry he imagines himself to be, he is soon overcome by a taste for home comfort. As Nizan ironically observes: '[il] ne tenait pas à changer de prison'(**19**). Bernard is trapped, but the complicity is essential.

Having described the attempts to establish the conspiracy of *La Guerre civile* in the first part of the novel, Nizan turns his attention to the major counter-conspiracy in the second. As though to point his reader in the right direction, he takes stock of Bernard's position in a long, omniscient description which is ironic but not without sympathy. Once again the hindsight is significant:

> Parce qu'il passe presque toutes ses journées rue d'Ulm, où à la Sorbonne, ou dans les rues, dans les cafés, en compagnie de camarades qu'il pense avoir librement choisis, parce qu'il tente d'organiser une vie qui ait peu de communications avec l'avenue Mozart, Bernard Rosenthal a l'illusion de demeurer entièrement étranger aux soucis et aux plaisirs pour lesquels vivent les siens. Comment un jeune homme échapperait-il à une illusion si agréable, qui le dispense si vite de résoudre les difficiles problèmes de la classe, de la complicité et du sang?
> Mais Bernard voit assez souvent sa famille à l'heure du dîner, qu'il partage avec elle quatre ou cinq jours par semaine avenue Mozart, il passe avec elle une partie de ses vacances, et la mensualité que lui verse son père lui permet de ne pas toucher à l'argent qu'il a hérité de sa grand-mère paternelle: de toutes les façons, il n'aurait pas à chercher les moyens de gagner ses études et son pain. Il a beau refuser à son père la moindre reconnaissance, trouver que cette pension lui est bien due, et que c'est toujours autant de repris sur la bourgeoisie au compte de la Révolution, ces arrangements d'argent et ces rencontres maintiennent encore peu à peu près tous les liens qu'il croit avoir intérieurement rompus; comme c'est facile, une rupture intérieure, qu'aucune action n'atteste que la satisfaction du cœur!(**133-4**)

Nizan might have added that this bond which holds Bernard still to the family allows him to pursue that most bourgeois of escapades, an affair. Furthermore, since it is with his sister-in-law, it underlines the enclosed, inward-looking nature of the world from which he is powerless to escape. On the point of death he describes it as '[une] union pareille à un inceste permis'(237) and it invites an interesting comparison with the earlier episode with his sister in Naxos (140-51). Laforgue's remark after an evening he has spent dining with the Rosenthal family is, as ever, directly and ironically relevant: '—Vous faites rudement famille'(156).

Just as Bernard has been self-deluded about *La Guerre civile*, so he is about his relationship with Catherine. As we have seen, he believes his actions to be dictated by revolutionary idealism, but it takes little time for others to see them as romantic, irresponsible and self-indulgent. Régnier, whose own doubts perhaps allow him to be more instantly objective in his judgement, dismisses Rosenthal's project as 'Stupide, inefficace, toujours improvisé'(124); but in the end, others are no less perceptive. Four years earlier, Marie-Anne had considered her brother's youthful enthusiasms to be 'affreusement exotiques'(147). Subsequently Catherine accuses him on more than one occasion of behaving like a schoolboy: '—Tu as quinze ans [...] tu es un collégien'(187); '—Tu es comme les enfants' (205). But as on all occasions, Bernard is blind and driven on by what she calls 'Votre terrible orgueil' (229). His affair with her becomes all-consuming, a personal conspiracy against his fellow collaborators whom he forgets, as Laforgue realizes after his friend's death (245), and against his family: yet another 'guerre civile'. Even after the discovery of his affair with Catherine, he continues to delude himself to the point of imagining that suicide will be both a final gesture of his defiance and a sign of his integrity. But he underestimates the power the family can exert and the degree to which he remains its prisoner. From the moment he is confronted by the others, put on trial—'[le] tribunal familial' (226)—to his burial in the Père-Lachaise cemetery (Chapters XVIII-XX), the artificial and inexorable nature of the process in and by which he is caught is underlined. The scene of confrontation is a set-piece, the only way the family (and the society to which it belongs) knows how to deal with the matter. It also resembles the opening scene of a play:

> Les circonstances sentaient trop le drame pour qu'on eût
> allumé toutes les lampes; le grand salon était plongé dans
> la pénombre comme s'il y avait une panne de secteur,
> qu'on eût apporté de l'office une seule lampe. Et au fond
> de cette demi-nuit domestique où les radiateurs cognaient,
> comme une exilée de la jeunesse, de l'été, dans une robe
> bleu pâle, Catherine était assise, la nuque sur le bois
> cannelé du canapé; elle avait croisé les jambes, ses bas
> brillaient, elle fumait. (222-3)

Bernard reflects, with more relevance than he realizes: 'On
est dans le drame'(223). Each participant plays his or her
expected role: M. Rosenthal storms from the room without
speaking; Claude makes a threatening gesture; Mme
Rosenthal has the principal part and leads the action;
Catherine speaks only to dismiss Bernard. At the close of the
chapter, it is as if the tension breaks, marked by a series of past
historics, and the scene has come to an end: 'Tout le monde
commença à bouger, Catherine décroisa ses jambes et ses
doigts, s'abandonna contre le dossier, ferma les yeux. Claude
embrassa sa mère, Bernard sortit'(227). But this is not the end
of the play; it will go on, and increasingly have a tragic
inevitability about it. Bernard is caught: 'une espèce de grande
machine s'était mise en movement, [...] il aurait beau essayer
d'arrêter ses bielles il ne l'empêcherait plus de tourner'(228-9).
At no time should we forget, however, that Bernard is not
simply an innocent victim of circumstances, but rather, or at
least as much, of himself. Catherine is close to the truth when
she comments that: 'Ce drame est arrivé parce que vous l'avez
voulu'(229-30). And this is what causes events to slip from
something approaching genuine tragedy to melodrama, what
Bernard himself describes as 'un drame bourgeois, du mauvais
Diderot'(227). Thus, after the family has passed judgement, he
continues in his pathetic pursuit of Catherine until, faced by her
rejection of his advances, he decides to kill himself. But his
suicide is not the noble act of ultimate defiance that he
imagines, rather a squalid, melodramatic cliché more suited to
a run-of-the-mill detective novel: 'Bernard voulut se lever,
courir, se délivrer du poison, mais il n'arriva qu'à glisser de son
lit et atteindre sans même se redresser, s'agenouiller, l'entrée
de la salle de bains où il s'enlisa enfin dans les vases gluantes
du sommeil'(237). Fittingly, in keeping with the same literary
'tradition', his corpse is discovered the following morning by

the concierge. Nor does the drama cease there. Mme
Rosenthal watches over her son's corpse in her 'grand deuil
théâtral'(240) and the burial ceremony in Père-Lachaise is
described by Bloyé as 'du bon théâtre'(241). (We should note in
passing the heavily ironic note Nizan will introduce by
situating the family tomb *au-dessus* du Mur des Fédérés' [240;
my italics].) Only then does the drama end: 'tout était établi
dans l'ordre de la mort'(237). Rosenthal has finally rejoined 'le
sein des Familles [qui] n'en lâcheront rien'(242) and Nizan's
earlier comment comparing the world to a jellyfish (30) is
appropriately repeated in a slightly different but equally
sinister form:

> Comme c'est puissant et inflexible, une famille! C'est
> tranquille comme un corps, comme un organe qui bouge
> à peine, qui respire rêveusement jusqu'au moment des
> périls, mais c'est plein de secrets, de ripostes latentes,
> d'une fureur et d'une rapidité biologiques, comme une
> anémone de mer au fond d'un pli de granit, tranquille,
> nonchalante, inconsciente comme une fleur, qui laisse
> flotter ses tentacules gorge de pigeon, en attendant de les
> renfermer sur un crabe, une crevette, une coquille qui
> coule ...(229)

From start to finish, therefore, Rosenthal is seen to have been
part of a system from which escape is impossible even through
death. Yet another conspiracy, perhaps the most powerful of
all, has been set in motion to replace all others, and it seems as
though the same process could go on indefinitely. Even though
they are used in a slightly different context, Bernard's earlier
words in his letter to Laforgue—'nous vivons à l'intérieur de la
bourgeoisie'(83)—provide an admirable summary of his
predicament

Were *La Conspiration* to be no more than the story of
Bernard Rosenthal, we would read it as an indictment of the
family and the way it can conspire to exert pressure to conform
to certain pre-established values, on the one hand, and as a
rueful acknowledgement of the impracticability of youthful
idealism and a pessimistic reflection on the impossibility of
individual action on the other. But it is more complex than that.
Through the relationships between the principal characters,
the introduction of secondary ones (Carré, Régnier and

Massart), and various stylistic and formal devices, Nizan takes
the discussion and its implications considerably further.

The first of these relationships is the one between Rosenthal
and Pluvinage. While the former is socially privileged and likes
to impose himself as a leader ('voix prophetique'[12]; 'faisait
figure de chef'[72]; 'ne se plaisait qu'à donner des conseils, des
avertissements'[108]), Pluvinage is self-effacing and solitary,
and has grown up 'dans le monde qui se voue à l'élimination
des déchets urbains et à l'enregistrement des catastrophes
privées'(268). From the opening scene it is clear that, for some
reason, Pluvinage is the outsider within the group. When he
leaves his friends they 'se sentirent légèrement soulagés par
son départ'(23) and later Rosenthal 'se défiait vaguement de
Pluvinage'(72). His name invites mockery (72). Socially he is far
inferior to Rosenthal and his single, rented room in the rue
Cujas is 'assez sinistre'(23). According to Régnier, he is 'assez
louche'(216). Physically he is dominated by his mistress
Marguerite, who is 'virile'(42) and 'un peu plus grande que
[lui]' (263). In most respects he is a mirror image or inversion of
Rosenthal, but in the end they are both subject to the same
kinds of formative circumstances, what Pluvinage justly calls
his 'affreuse fatalité'.

Although we have to wait for his confession before we know
for certain that Pluvinage has betrayed Carré to the police, we
are left with little doubt about his guilt. At the same time, as
Rosenthal and Laforgue have to recognize when they decide to
interrogate him, suspicion has to be balanced against the fact
that Pluvinage is the only member of the group to have
followed the logic of what they believe to be their political
convictions by joining the Communist Party. He denies their
accusations of betrayal, yet on evidence that is no more than
impressionistic and circumstantial ('sans l'ombre d'une preuve
réelle'[221]), they decide to denounce him. Days later, and with
an irony of which he is quite unaware, Rosenthal remarks:
'cette dénonciation ne nous a paru étrange que parce que nous
pensions au caractère phénoménal de Pluvinage, mais il y a
sans doute beaucoup à dire sur son caractère intelligible. Qui
n'est pas double?'(221).

In the first two chapters of the final section of the novel,
related essentially from Pluvinage's point of view, his betrayal
will be confirmed and to some extent explained, though it will
not be more fully explored until his *récit* in Chapter XXIII.

Faced by the suspicions of his Party comrades, he withdraws into an isolation ('la solitude parfaite'[254]) from which there can be no escape or salvation: 'Il était entièrement sans espoir, il savait que la trahison est irrémédiable comme la mort, et que, comme la mort, elle ne s'efface jamais'(255). He confesses to Marguerite, is violently slapped by her, and after she has fled, falls asleep—not unlike Bernard earlier in the novel (23)— 'épuisé par sa métamorphose'(264). Pluvinage is frequently likened to Lange in Le Cheval de Troie, and is regularly associated with images based on night, water and death. It is no coincidence that, when he leaves his cell meeting to return to the rue Cujas, the night should be ' visqueuse'(255) and that his walk should take him across the area bordering the canal Saint-Martin and the hôpital Saint-Louis:

> Pluvinage descendit le trottoir de gauche de la rue de la Grange-aux-Belles le long du mur de l'hôpital Saint-Louis. Il faisait assez froid, mais il ne gelait pas, c'était simplement un temps humide et éventé. Quai de Jemmapes, le vent sifflait dans les branches des arbres le long du canal et le reflet de Paris illuminait le plafond bas des nuages. Serge releva le col de son pardessus et longea la berge.(254)

As we noted earlier, these qualities are associated in Le Cheval de Troie with systems of oppression and in particular with the forces of Fascism. In La Conspiration, they resurface in the descriptions of the police commissioner, Massart. Massart's eyes are like those of a fish 'd'une transparence aveugle, impénétrable'(256); he exudes '[une] cordialité huilée'(256), and indulges in 'un bavardage où il noyait ses amis et ceux qu'il interrogeait'(257). His office overlooks 'l'eau lente du bras du fleuve' and 'un cortège de voitures et d'autos'(257).

In his récit, Pluvinage explains his behaviour as a consequence of his rejection by the others and by Rosenthal and Laforgue in particular. Their intellectual superiority and academic success make him violently envious. But envy soon gives way to a feeling of total humiliation, and his response at failing to win a place at the École normale supérieure is visceral: 'l'échec m'humiliait mortellement. Je me disais enfin que c'était dans l'ordre, que j'irais rejoindre ma famille dans quelque destinée humide et noire d'insecte de la pourriture et du bois, que je serais rejeté dans son univers'(279). Joining the

Communist party is therefore less an expression of political conviction than a means to gain credibility and even revenge. The effect is immediate: 'Vous étiez stupéfaits, humiliés. Vous aviez enfin quelque chose à m'envier, un acte auquel vous n'osiez encore vous résoudre'(282). Membership also brings Pluvinage the experience of non-judgmental comradeship, a sense of belonging and a conviction which is remarkably similar to Carré's belief that Communism is 'un style de vie' (211): 'on ne guérit pas du communisme quand on l'a vécu ...' (283), he says. Faced with the attacks on communist institutions by the government and the police, however, his convictions waver: 'J'avais adhéré à un corps promis à la victoire, il me paraissait impossible de m'associer à une défaite'. And he continues with a statement which anticipates his subsequent behaviour and potential fascist inclinations: 'Les gens comme moi ne doivent être capables de fidélité qu'avec les vainqueurs' (288). He is a ready prey for Massart.

Yet for Pluvinage, Massart is more than just an embodiment of law and order Several nights after discovering that Carré is in hiding with Régnier, Pluvinage dreams that he has already denounced him: 'Je m'éveillai un matin sur un rêve: je venais de dénoncer la retraite de Carré à un homme qui avait tantôt les traits de mon père, tantôt mon propre visage'(293). Pluvinage's father had become 'chef de bureau des inhumations à la direction des affaires municipales et du contentieux'(266). In his office, as Serge[18] recalls, hung 'sages aquarelles, [...] des vues de cimetières et de chapelles généralement représentées sous un ciel d'automne avec des feuilles mortes dans tous les coins'(266). Surrounded by the whole paraphernalia of burial and death, the child, became obsessed by it and cut out pictures of 'des modèles de catafalques, de corbillards et de caveaux' (266). Massart's office in the Préfecture de Police is situated in the same area of Paris where Pluvinage's father had worked, and is described by his son as one of the city's 'îles de la mort, [...] ces divers domaines qui sont nommément ceux de la maladie, de la police et de la mort' (268). When he eventually

---

[18] It is curious that of the main characters, Serge Pluvinage is the one whose forename Nizan uses most frequently. Is this to make an oblique reference to Trotskyist intellectual and novelist Victor Serge (the choice of poet Jules Laforgue's surname might be similar), or to underline the class distinction between him and Rosenthal? (It might further be noted that Bernard's family's obsession with money is reflected in the surname Rosenthal, the last syllable evocative of the German silver Thaler.)

goes there to denounce Carré, mental pictures of the two men suddenly fuse: 'je me perdis dans des couloirs gris et ternes qui ressemblaient à des couloirs d'hôpital: je me précipitais les yeux fermés jusqu'au fond de mon enfance, mon père allait ouvrir la première de ces portes vitrées, je reverrais ses aquarelles funéraires sur les murs'(295-6).

Clearly there is in this relationship a search for a father-substitute on Serge's part (Massart has also probably been his mother's lover), and some critics have seen in his attraction to the police chief hints of homosexuality. But more significant is the way all three men are linked by the worlds of night and death. Pluvinage, like Rosenthal, is completely conditioned and trapped by his formative years, and only momentarily glimpses an escape. Just as Rosenthal had enjoyed real freedom perhaps for the only time when he visited his sister in Naxos, Pluvinage had glimpsed an alternative to his dreary existence in a brief flirtation with his young cousin, Jeanne (273-9). For each of the two young men, these experiences constitute a transition from adolescence to adulthood. To be sure their lives thereafter take different directions, but each ends in betrayal, failure and death: literally in the case of Rosenthal, metaphorically in that of Pluvinage. The latter's words of despair could equally apply to them both: 'Toute ma vie est faite de ces avortements'(275).

In contrast we have Laforgue. Of the three he is the least developed, but he is vital to their relationship and is in a privileged position. He corresponds with Rosenthal, has access to his friend's papers, reads Pluvinage's *récit* and, as has been mentioned, also acts on a number of occasions as an alternative to Nizan's own omniscient authorial voice. This is self-evident from the start. While he is clearly more active than Rosenthal in the day-to-day organization of *La Guerre civile*, there is no sense that in the long term he is any more committed. From the first, he expresses a degree of healthy scepticism: 'À la rentrée, dit Laforgue, nous pourrons donc publier cette revue, puisqu'il se trouve des philanthropes assez naïfs pour nous confier des argents qu'ils ne reverront pas. Nous la publierons, et au bout d'un certain temps, elle mourra...'(13). He counters Rosenthal's idea that 'la victoire dans la pensée' (64) will lead automatically to success, and that what matters is 'la violence théorique'(64), with caution and realism: 'Crois-tu que ce soit de notre théorie que les masses attendent d'être pénétrées?'(64).

While this critical role is essential, it is not until the final chapter that he assumes a new significance in his own right. Before this we see and learn little of him. As a student at the École normale supérieure, he fashionably conceals his academic brilliance behind a show of indifference; he frequents local cafés and enjoys the occasional affair with a prostitute. He has a more long-term relationship with Pauline and uses her to facilitate Rosenthal's plan to have Simon moved, but she is no more than an object for his entertainment or scorn. Their relationship remains sexually unconsummated and the nearest he gets to satisfying her is by masturbation (39). This 'failure' may be significant (like Pluvinage's), an early sign that he too has yet to pass from adolescence to adulthood (302), a passage which he conceives as being analogous to a primitive ritual. For him, however, this transition is achieved not by any ceremony, but by illness: 'La maladie intervint dans la vie de Laforgue et remplit pour lui l'office de sorcier. On ne pense presque jamais que les maladies arrangent tout, qu'on se transforme, qu'on médite dans ces fuites et ces sommeils où tout est suspendu dans l'attente du retour, du réveil' (303). For days he remains in a coma, 'dans de profonds sommeils moites et noirs' (305), a description which reminds us both of the worlds frequented by Pluvinage (and also by Massart and his father) and of Rosenthal's suicide. But unlike them, Laforgue resurfaces; his childhood and adolescence are behind him and it is as though he is reborn:

> Il songeait qu'il venait de naître, que sa maladie avait été sa seconde naissance, la naissance qu'il avait passion-nément espérée. Tout était consumé, son enfance, son adolescence, il existait, il avait commencé à exister pour la première fois à la seconde même où il s'était réveillé dans la nuit de la clinique sous la lumière bleue. Et il avait commencé en même temps à marcher vers sa mort, après le sursis de vingt-deux ans qui s'était étendu entre sa première naissance et sa grande maladie, après cette parenthèse où le temps perdu ne tirait point à conséquence. (307)

To an important and it seems intended degree, Laforgue succeeds where Rosenthal and Pluvinage have failed or have been defeated. His recovery is not simply from illness and near death but from the conditioning influence of his social and educational environment. More significant still is his now fully lucid acceptance of death and purposeful attitude to his (new) life, a realization of his early determination to be 'absolument délivré de la peur de mourir'(13). But a problem remains. Laforgue is 'encore trop faible pour se révolter, il bougeait à peine'(308) and, even more menacingly, the family is still in evidence: 'ce monde où les gens qui vous aiment le mieux vous demandent compte de votre existence'(308). Before he has time fully to recover, Laforgue appears to be in danger of being reabsorbed and we should not forget his description of the group's anticipated future, which coincides with the date of the novel's composition. Once again the dual perspective must affect our reading. Whatever Nizan's optimism in the late 1920s was, and however fulfilling he would find his own role as a militant during the next decade, he now seems, in 1938, to be unable to hide his disappointment («Nous n'irons pas très loin» [301]) at having been trapped. This is not to say that optimism is diminished, but that optimism has still to find expression through meaningful action. At the close of *La Conspiration* we are left with the impression that the conspiracies of life, society and its multifarious systems (the 'amas [...] de gélatine'[30]) have proved too strong, and individuals either complicit with them or powerless to resist.

Early in the novel, Nizan comments omnisciently on the pressures which the previous generation tried to bring to bear, and on the dangers of succumbing to them:

> Tout allait-il donc recommencer? Allaient-ils être finalement contraints, après avoir appelé tous les naufrages qui conviennent aux grands siècles décoratifs, de naviguer, en observant les instructions nautiques et tous les signaux rouges des ponts, sur les eaux de plaine de la vie bourgeoise? (68)

On reflection, these words have an ominous ring to them.

Political cyphers

When Léon-Pierre Quint reviewed *La Conspiration* in the December 1938 issue of *Les Volontaires,* he criticized Nizan for

having characters who were 'insuffisamment individualisés'. It
is difficult not to agree. We know very little about the physical
appearance of the principal characters, about their dress or
their mannerisms. Nizan's concern is primarily to present them
as enactors of different states of mind or emotions. If this is
true of them then it is even more so of the trio Régnier, Carré
and Massart. They have limited roles, but are central in that
each in turn voices and exemplifies the ideological views which
are central to the novel, and which Nizan is inviting his readers
to compare.

Of the three, Régnier is the most tormented, a fact instantly
reflected in the brief physical description we are given of him:
'un homme long, un peu voûté, avec des yeux bleus qui se
déplaçaient avec une mobilité si grande qu'on croyait parfois
qu'il louchait, et un front nu qui lui donnait un air légèrement
égaré'(76). This man whom Rosenthal counts as a friend, and
of whom he speaks as 'l'homme le plus intelligent que je
connaisse'(79), is generally considered to have been modelled
on Barbusse, even though in 1928 he gives his age as thirty-
eight (Barbusse would have been fifty-five). If this is correct, it
invites an interesting reflection by Nizan on his role in the
Monde affair. It recalls the problem of what was considered at
the time to have been Barbusse's—or *Monde's*—ideological
weaknesses, has echoes of Nizan's grudging admiration for the
man and, most interestingly from the perspective of 1938,
offers a distinct critical commentary on the revolutionary zeal
of the group and of Rosenthal in particular. Régnier records
this in the extracts from his 'carnet noir' (Chapter X). The visit
which the young men pay to him (Chapter VI) is strained and
seemingly pointless, and Régnier reflects: 'tous les jeunes gens
me paraissent odieux'(121); 'ils ne feront que rêver'(125);
'Cette jeunesse passe son temps dans un état de songe; elle est
assez comblée par la fabrication de ses symboles et de ses
signes. [...] Ses actions n'ont pas un coefficient de réalité très
élevé'(127). And, like Laforgue, he is critical of Rosenthal's
egoism and lack of concern for Simon. Régnier's notes also
resonate with references to the inevitability of old age and
death, and with despair over the difficulty, if not the
impossibility, of achieving anything permanent either through
action or through writing. Reflecting on the ambiguity of *sens*
(direction or meaning), he writes:

> La situation fondamentale de la vie consiste à ne
> pouvoir jamais revenir vers un carrefour toujours
> dépassé et toujours imaginaire de chances et de choix: tous
> les chemins vont dans le même sens. Cette situation est
> moins angoissante qu'absurde, elle ne supporte point
> d'être pensée.
> On a toujours voulu dans un absurde esprit de
> calembour sur le *sens* substituer une *signification* à une
> *direction*. Mais l'existence n'est en relation avec rien.
> Toute l'intelligence échoue à découvrir un rapport de
> signification dans la direction unique de la vie vers la
> mort. (128)

It is possible that with remarks such as these Nizan is
offering a critique of Barbusse, or at least of what he still
considers to be the fundamental defeatism of the older man's
generation. Régnier's own reply to his self-admonition
'Retarder la mort par la fureur'(129) is, after all, 'Je suis trop
paresseux pour la colère'(130). But, given the obsessive
presence of references to death in his own writing, these
'extraits' may surely be read as much if not more as an
autocritique by Nizan, or as a statement of frustration or
despair at his *own* achievements: 'Roman. Comment décrire
un homme ou un monde qui changent avec des moyens assez
efficaces pour donner à la description des chances de durée.
N'écrivons plus'(126).

Situated at the very end of the first part of *La Conspiration*,
these 'extraits d'un carnet noir' offer a commentary and issue a
challenge. The rest of the novel, in which the various
conspiracies unfold and in which death is predominant, is an
illustration of the gloomy fatalism and pessimism which colour
them. It is almost as though Nizan decided to place them at this
juncture in the story in the full knowledge of what was to come.
But the problem of uncertainty remains, and is what lies behind
the appearances of Carré and Massart.

While Régnier may be modelled on Barbusse, Carré is
thought by some to be inspired by Vaillant-Couturier (even
though the politician is also referred to directly on two
occasions [209; 287]). Vaillant-Couturier was arrested in
September 1929, a month before the fictional arrest of Carré.
We learn very little about the latter, and even his name
suggests that he is little more than emblematic. We know that
he has sought shelter from persecution by the police with

Régnier, alongside whom he had fought in the First World
War. They are therefore of the same generation. Physically he
has even less presence than Régnier; all we learn is that (no
doubt significantly) he is taller than the police officer who
arrests him. He is completely unperturbed by what happens;
we are told nothing of its consequences, and in terms of the
novel's plot his appearance in Chapter XVII would be entirely
arbitrary were it not that it allows the 'trials' of Pluvinage and
Rosenthal to be closely associated. His real significance,
however, lies in what we learn about his beliefs and the way
these are contrasted with Régnier's doubts and vacillations.
We are informed by the narrator that for Carré, Communism is
'la conscience même qu'il avait de lui-même et de sa vie'(210).
For Régnier he represents '[la] coïncidence d'une politique et
d'un destin, cet agencement qu'il désespérait d'atteindre jamais
entre l'histoire et l'homme'(211), and on which he reflects in his
diary. If, in Chapter X, Nizan has already offered a critique of
Régnier's position, now, through Carré, he extends it and
more importantly voices the positive alternative. Régnier is
and will remain weak because he is incapable of seeing beyond
the personal to the collective. What he defines as the
intellectual freedom to criticise, to refuse discipline, is in fact a
limitation, an inability to see the whole as the sum of individual
parts. Carré has to spell out to him that Communism is in this
respect a faith: individual differences have to be subsumed in
the interest of totality. That is what gives it its power: 'Le
communisme est une politique, c'est aussi un style de vie. C'est
pourquoi l'Église nous redoute et nous mesure sans cesse, [...]
elle sait que le communisme joue comme elle sur la certitude
d'une victoire absolument totale'(211). Only when this is
understood and practised will true progress be possible.
Socialism fails because it falls short of this absolute: 'Les
socialistes se réunissent et parlent politique, élections, et après,
c'est fini, ça ne commande pas leur respiration, leur vie privée,
leurs fidélités personnelles, leur idée de la mort, de l'avenir'
(212). Communism, on the contrary, succeeds for Carré
precisely because it offers a vision, a system which absorbs
individual and occasional doubts, or 'inflexions politiques d'un
jour'(213); it creates 'un rapport total avec d'autres hommes'.
Régnier begins to grasp that this may be 'un monde dur et
enviable où il ne lui semblait toujours pas possible d'entrer'
(213).

The left-wing positions adopted by Régnier and Carré clearly represent those to which Nizan and his generation were exposed, and which many adopted. There is no doubt as to where the author's own preference lies. Communism, for Carré as it was for Nizan, is indeed a faith: it permeates his whole being and way of life. But as in the case of Laforgue's new resolve at the close of the novel, it remains untested; we do not see his conviction translated into meaningful action. For this reason the alternative is necessary, a view which rejects the notion of historical progress and of collective action based on shared conviction in favour of chance and coincidence. This, as Massart explains to Pluvinage, is the basis for influence and power:

> Le secret de la police, [...] c'est qu'*il n'y a pas d'histoire.*
> Tous les professeurs ont menti, tous. Il n'existe pas de
> forces qui travaillent à faire l'histoire. Les académiciens
> parlent des forces spirituelles et les marxistes des forces de
> l'économie [...]. De petites chances et de petits hommes
> fabriquent les grands événements. [...] Tout le monde
> ignore les coulisses de la chance et le secret des petits
> hommes.(258-9)

Such a philosophy creates the illusion of power and is what momentarily seduces a Pluvinage eager for revenge and desperate to erase his sense of humiliation. But there is something Mephistophelian about it. Massart explains that this kind of individual, isolated behaviour is a form of death: 'on entre dans la police comme on se suicide'(260). And this is exactly what Pluvinage does, recognising in the final paragraph of his *récit* how misguided he has been only when it is too late:

> Il est dur de penser que les communistes avaient
> raison, que je n'ai pas seulement trahi des hommes
> détestés, mais la vérité et l'espoir. Vous m'avez tout
> appris de votre vérité, je puis la combattre, mais je ne
> peux plus être dupe des mensonges qu'on dresse contre
> elle. L'homme qui veut jouer l'histoire est toujours joué,
> on ne change rien par des petits moyens. La révolution est
> *le contraire* de la police.(299)

The final message of *La Conspiration* seems therefore to be quite unambiguous. But if Communism is to triumph it demands resolve, and will not be without cost. Rosenthal is literally dead, Pluvinage metaphorically so, and Laforgue only just survives. As we have seen, his rite of passage through illness is symbolic and significant, but it is only an initiation.

Form and style

Just as in terms of its content La Conspiration is the most complex and ambiguous of Nizan's novels, so in its structural organization and style it is the most varied and adventurous. The plots of both Antoine Bloyé and Le Cheval de Troie have a sequential, linear thread (modified by recapitulation, in the case of the first) which draws the reader forward to the author's intended goal. In both novels Nizan's principal narrative voice is that of the omniscient author, allowing him both to reproduce his characters' innermost private thoughts and to intervene in order to comment or to situate his characters in a sociohistorical or political context which, if necessary, may go beyond to the present. He interprets at will, draws conclusions and even dictates the kind of response he intends his reader to have. This he continues to do in La Conspiration, in spite of a more varied range of narrative modes: diary, letters, confession for example. As author-narrator he has access to all of these. As in the earlier novels too, the action moves forward, albeit irregularly, and the time span (June 1928 to December 1929) is carefully charted.[19]

On two occasions Nizan also dips into and describes events from the past; in Chapter IV (45-57) we have the description of the transportation of Jaurès's ashes to the Panthéon, and in Chapter XI the account of Bernard's idyllic holiday in Naxos with his sister. Each of these retrospective digressions is important for the novel's overall development. In the first, the young men turn away from what is essentially a bourgeois ceremony and in so doing already show themselves to be incapable of challenging the society which produced it and of coming to terms with the beginnings of the political changes that would culminate a decade later in the Popular Front. In

---

[19] As Adèle King has observed (op. cit., p. 146, n. 25), there are minor slips in Nizan's chronology but they are not serious.

the second, as we have already noted, Rosenthal indulges himself in a moment of escape in preference to any engagement with political activity, however much he may like to talk about revolution to his sister. Each of these episodes is self-contained, and elsewhere there are cameo descriptions in Nizan's best journalistic style, for example his account of Parisians in their *résidences secondaires* in Normandy. But there are also not a few occasions in the novel when Nizan appears guilty of self-indulgence or over-elaboration. While Pauline may ultimately serve Rosenthal's plans to have Simon moved to a more important military headquarters, there seems little justification for the length of the scene in Chapter IV between her and Laforgue. Similarly, not only is the account of Simon's spying overlong, but his relationship with Gladys is only relevant in as much as it allows Nizan to fill out his satiric description of military life and its values.

In isolation such moments have to be considered weaknesses, but on closer examination they may also be seen as exaggerated examples of an irregular and episodic construction which is basic to the novel as a whole. Chapters vary greatly in length (from three pages to thirty-five) and each one is subdivided into sections of different lengths so as to create at times the impression that Nizan is assembling a kind of mosaic, and that he is incapable of sustaining a continuous discursive narrative. This fragmentation within the overall structure of the book is also repeated in the variety of stylistic devices Nizan employs. We have the cursory notes of Régnier's *cahier noir*, the interior monologue of Pluvinage's *récit* (the only time when the omniscient author's voice and that of a character fuse), the dramatic tone of the opening or several of the dialogues, the mock-heroic descriptions of the young men: 'Ils sortirent du jardin pour aller boire et ils avaient le choix parmi tous les cafés qu'il y a entre la place du Panthéon et le Jardin des Plantes'(14). Throughout, the flat, neutral formulae inherited from the traditional nineteenth-century novel ('C'était un jour de pluie du commencement d'avril...'[72]; 'M. Édouard Rosenthal était un homme lourd, aux joues molles...' [134]) are offset by passages of poetic fancy or by those in which Nizan appears to want to create effect by an accumulation of details. Sometimes this is successful. For Simon, 'le défilé étrange de la vie'(118), which he observes after his release from prison has the strong, visual qualities of a prose poem:

... il regarda longtemps passer, à travers les bureaux de la petite porte du corps de garde, des ouvriers, des filles en cheveux, des clochards, des camions, des fardiers, des femmes qui poussaient des voitures d'enfant le long des acacias en fleur du chemin de fer de Ceinture [...]. De l'autre côté de la cour, la zone s'étendait avec ses fumées pauvres, ses arbustes en fleurs qui fusaient sur les pancartes de brocanteurs, les annonces des restaurants, les huttes africaines de tôle, de planches et de carton; des filles décoiffées piétinaient dans la poussière blanche du printemps, les bas sur les chevilles, des enfants à moitié nus jouaient avec de vieilles roues de bicyclettes sur un terrain de pierrailles, de gravats, de chiffons consumés, de boîtes de conserve et de ressorts de sommier; les clochers noirs, les cheminées hérissaient le triste pays natal des Parisiens. (118-9)

Equally effective is the description of life in Normandy (163) or of the two Jewish communities (traditional and assimilated) in Paris (19). But the technique may be overdone. In the description of the arrival of Jaurès's cortège at the Panthéon, what might have been dramatic in a newspaper article in which he develops the image of the flow of life-blood ('On ne pouvait penser qu'à des puissances drues, à la sève, à un fleuve, au cours du sang. Le boulevard méritait soudain son nom d'artère' [55]), seems exaggerated and over-stylized in a novel. In this same passage Nizan incongruously invokes the Flight from Egypt: 'On pensait naturellement au passage de la mer Rouge et sans doute le président du Conseil n'était-il pas beaucoup plus fier que Moïse, avec ce Pharaon et ses chars de guerre qui lui galopaient sur les talons et les deux murailles liquides qui s'impatientaient si longtemps miraculeuses, et avait-il hâte d'être arrivé sur la rive du Panthéon'(53-4).

We also have to recognize that in a novel which, for all its irony and elements of *autocritique*, still has an ideological message to convey, Nizan continues to comment and to direct his reader's attention. To be sure his intrusions are less substantial than in *Le Cheval de Troie*, but they remain numerous and wide-ranging. Thus he comments at will on such diverse matters as 'des dames entre deux âges'(12), the young bourgeois intellectual exemplified by Laforgue (18), the young and their obsession with death (26), the gullibility and social pretensions of army officers (116), what Bernard imagines his love for Catherine to be (235) or Pluvinage's or Laforgue's unvoiced thoughts (**234; 307**). His methods vary. Sometimes we find a shift from simple description to aphoristic comment. Thus the thumbnail sketch of Édouard Rosenthal closes with the sentence: 'On ne peut consentir à vivre qu'en ignorant tout du style de sa mort et des formes de son vieillissement'(**134**). Not infrequently, the description of something specific becomes a generalisation. Of Bernard, Nizan writes: 'Il était d'une génération où l'on confondait presque toujours les succès de l'amour avec ceux d'une insurrection'(**223**). Of Laforgue: 'Il généralise un peu vite ses expériences'(**43**). Of the group as a whole: 'Ils ne savaient pas encore comme c'est lourd et mou le monde...'(**30**). On the uncertainty and impressionability of young people like Simon: 'Que de cascades d'influences, de jeux de reflets sur des glaces, dans la vie des jeunes gens qui se sentent un peu trop invertébrés encore pour marcher sans compagnons, sans confidents et sans témoins'(**96**). And of the same character just before he breaks open the cupboard containing the documents: 'Il était bien de son âge: il n'arrivait pas à croire que les actions de jeunesse pussent entraîner des conséquences'(**111**).

Nizan also regularly hides behind the impersonal *on*, not simply as a descriptive device ('On était au début de juin, il faisait tout à fait beau'[**118**]), but again to generalize or to moralize: 'Il fallait que Bernard crût que Catherine mentait: il pouvait confondre des mensonges, mais non l'oubli. On vainc les maladies, non la mort'(**230**). Similarly we find 'On raconte toujours son enfance à la femme qu'on doit aimer'(**170**); and 'On ne peut pas dire qu'ils soient absolument dupes de leurs discours sur la métamorphose du monde'(**30**).

As in his earlier novels Nizan blatantly uses authorial intervention to remind his readers of the importance of the historical perspective we discussed earlier. He underlines his protagonists' immaturity for example: 'ils ignorent tout de la vie que mènent les hommes [...] il n'y a encore au fond de leur politique que des métaphores et des cris...'(**30**). He looks back to a time when 'la France avait alors pour grands hommes le président Poincaré...'(**45**). Reflecting on international events and on the massacres in Palestine in 1928, he writes: 'ces tueries étonnaient encore des hommes qui devaient, sept ou huit ans plus tard, s'accoutumer avec une effrayante souplesse aux extraordinaires massacres d'Abyssinie, de Chine, d'Espagne' (**178**). Bernard is immature: 'Dix ans plus tard, Bernard n'aurait pas fait de projets, il se fût sans doute senti assuré de l'emporter par la patience'(191).

Finally, what is particularly striking about *La Conspiration* and what to a large extent counterbalances and even justifies some of these features is its thematic coherence. As we have already noted, while they are not as obsessively present as in *Le Cheval de Troie*, where they are metaphorically vital as a vehicle for the political issues which are being discussed, references to death—and in Laforgue's case, to the possibility of rebirth—make *La Conspiration* as much a philosophical work as a sociopolitical one. It offers a reflection on life in which chance and arbitrariness appear to be decisive (as Massart argues), but whose direction is in fact already determined from the outset if not before. While individuals— and this is obviously true in Rosenthal's case—may believe that they are in control and can exercise their free will, they are in fact merely playing bit parts in some vast drama. This is particularly apparent in the relationship between Rosenthal and Catherine, where Nizan bases his description of it quite precisely on metaphors relating to the theatre and theatrical posturing. But it soon becomes apparent that this metaphor or analogy can be extended to the action of the novel as a whole, at which point the fragmented and fractured nature of so much of the narration assumes a new relevance and significance. Life is made up of a series of largely discontinuous scenes or tableaux in which individuals come and go, and which are often no more than cyphers, extensions of their particular milieu, or are vehicles for Nizan's ideas. There is no need for them to be fully rounded, autonomous characters; they are in fact inauthentic, and deliberately so. Nizan shows them to have been consciously or unconsciously absorbed by the roles imposed on and expected of them. They inhabit self-contained, enclosed worlds and have adopted the costume or uniform of that world; they are both complicitous and victims.

Reception

In 1938, and by the time *La Conspiration* was published, Nizan was considered by many to be one of the French Communist Party's leading intellectuals, possibly the most respected and influential, and it is hardly surprising that when it appeared the novel should have received almost universal acclaim.[20] In fact the only serious hostile criticism came from Robert Brasillach in the extreme right-wing paper *Je suis partout* (9 December), who accused him of 'un érotisme assez sale' and, interestingly anticipating some of the accusations made against Nizan after his death, found in the 'récit de Pluvinage' a predilection for a behaviour 'qu'il a dû rencontrer au parti communiste ou ailleurs'. For André Rousseaux, in *Le Figaro* (29 October), and Robert Kemp, in *La Revue universelle* (1 December), Nizan was a writer of unquestionable talent but had wasted it by his affiliation with the Communist party. Occasionally, and not without an element of perverse delight perhaps, some right-wing critics also claimed to find in *La Conspiration* elements worthy of one of their own. René Bourget-Pailleron, for example, wrote in *La Revue des deux mondes* (1 January 1939) that the novel 'ressemble par moments à une satire d'un polémiste de droite contre les bourgeois révolutionnaires'. But even those ideologically opposed to Nizan recognized the strengths of the book. In *Axes* (14 October), Marcelle Gaston-Marin praised him as an astute psychological novelist and considered *La Conspiration* to be 'l'un des témoignages humains les plus pénétrants, si dur soit-il, de notre époque'. Robert de Traz, in *La Revue hebdomadaire* (10 December), read the novel as 'une satire très aiguë des normaliens d'aujourd'hui [*sic*], ou du moins de certains d'entre eux'; Georges Le Cardonnel, in *Le Journal* (20 November), dismissed his Communism as irrelevant: 'il paraît que M. Paul Nizan est communiste. Après la lecture de son livre, il semble qu'il soit avant tout romancier.'

---

[20] Most of what follows has been gleaned from M. Arpin, *La Fortune littéraire de Paul Nizan* (Berne, 1995).

As we might expect, the reviews in moderate or left-wing papers and periodicals were almost without exception favourable. Nizan was praised and admired for his psychological insight, his 'impitoyable lucidité', to use Claude Morgan's phrase in the *Cahiers du bolchévisme* (December), and his sincerity (Jean Cassou, *Commune*, January 1939). For Sartre (*NRF*, November). Nizan was 'un juge sans indulgence'. Morgan also argued in his review that the novel could and should be read as a warning against the arrogance of some intellectuals and as a plea for humility. Aragon, who only a few years later would spearhead the attacks against his former friend and colleague, wrote in *Europe* (December): 'Ce livre passionnant, où ce qui choque même a son prix, dont les défauts mêmes sont d'intérêt, pose des questions si brûlantes, et pour le roman et pour la vie, non point à la façon primitive des romanciers à thèse, mais par son existence même.' Several critics made the point that, unlike Nizan's previous novels and unlike many others written by Communists, *La Conspiration* was neither a social nor a socialist novel. Camus, in *Alger Républicain* (11 November), spoke for many when he claimed that Nizan managed not to 'sacrifier l'artiste au partisan'. The majority of reviewers were also favourable in their remarks about the novel's form. Only Kemp (in *La Revue universelle*) and Léon Marcanato (*Cahiers du Sud*, June 1939) considered the book to be ill-balanced. André Thérive, in *Le Temps* (20 October), made the point that the novel's fragmentation served precisely to 'simuler le désordre' and, while not drawing the same conclusions, Pierre Lœwel, in the right-wing *L'Ordre* (7 November), that 'l'ensemble légèrement fragmenté représente davantage un tableau stylisé qu'un tableau de la vie du siècle'.

No reviewer, however, highlighted—or at least discussed at any length—the two features of the novel which, as we have seen, give it its cohesion and uniqueness: the obsession with death and the images based on theatricality. Sartre, it is true, spoke of Nizan's description of a particular generation as of an 'âge artificiel' and 'âge inauthentique', but he failed to see how this is developed across the novel as a whole to become a comment on society and indeed on existence at large. Louis Parrot, in *Les Cahiers de la jeunesse* (15 October), recognized the theme of the rite of passage from adolescence to adulthood, but failed to consider how this was particularly relevant in the case of Laforgue and the problem that his recovery poses at the end of the novel, in relation to the significance of the struggle against death.

In subsequent years, and after the 'affaire Nizan',[21] *La Conspiration* has been read differently. For most critics the political element, while acknowledged, has been played down, though Annie Cohen-Solal's view that there is nothing militant about the novel is perhaps extreme.[22] Pascal Ory is more balanced, finding *La Conspiration* 'un livre qui approche la synthèse si rarement réussie entre les nécessités du discours politique (ici: «Que la révolte n'est pas la révolution») et celles de la création romanesque, nourrie d'aléatoire'.[23] Countering those of Nizan's attackers who saw in the novel a direct reflection of his disillusionment and 'liberal wishful thinking', Michael Scriven writes: '*La Conspiration* does not contain within it an implicit abandonment of communist ideology. On the contrary, this novel is a mature communist assessment of both an immature, pre-communist adolescent phase, and an immature, communist sectarian phase'; it is, to return more fully to his remark quoted earlier, 'a multi-faceted text in which a variety of alienated discourses are allowed scope to develop freely within a global framework that nonetheless remains resolutely communist.'[24] This last point is important. As has already been suggested, there is nothing in Nizan's activities or in his correspondence to suggest that at the time of writing *La Conspiration* he was other than a convinced and committed

---

[21] A good deal of attention has been paid to the 'affaire Nizan', and it may be that the whole truth has still to be revealed. After the outbreak of the Second World War, and Nizan's death (23 May 1940), Maurice Thorez accused him of having been a traitor, of having cultivated friends outside the Party, and of having collaborated with the bourgeois press for personal gain. Nizan's *Philosophies* collaborator Henri Lefebvre accused him, in his essay *L'Existentialisme* (1946), of treachery and of having been a police spy. Evidence for this was to be found, it was claimed, in his characterisation of Antoine Bloyé, Lange and Pluvinage. Aragon joined in the attack, and in *Les Communistes* (1946-1951) portrayed Nizan as Orfilat, a coward and a womaniser. Sartre took up the defence of his former friend, and, joined by other leading intellectuals, who included Camus, Paulhan and Aron, challenged the PCF to produce proof of their accusations; the challenge remained unanswered. Sartre used Nizan as the basis for his characters Schneider and Brunet in *Les Chemins de la liberté*, producing an image of a complex and even tormented left-wing intellectual. In 1960, in a preface to a new edition of *Aden Arabie*, he defended Nizan again, though he makes him appear more metaphysical and more of a romantic figure than he actually was.

[22] A. Cohen-Solal & H. Nizan, *op. cit.*, p. 226.

[23] *Nizan, Destin d'un révolté* (Paris, 1980), p. 159.

[24] Scriven, *op. cit.*, pp. 149, 158, respectively.

Communist. Indeed, in an interview with André Vemann in
Vendredi (8 December), Nizan observed:

> On n'a pas paru comprendre que le fait que j'étais
> communiste et celui que j'étais romancier ne soient pas
> inconciliables. Au contraire... Le communisme, comme
> toute expérience profonde, sert le romancier; précisément
> parce que le roman est instrument de connaissance et le
> communisme méthode de connaissance et d'expérience.

Yet given the matter of historical perspective discussed
earlier, the marginal nature of Carré as a voice of ideological
surety, and above all the irony and uncertainty which permeate
the text at almost every level, *La Conspiration* remains
troublesome and problematic. Nizan's planned sequel, *La
Soirée à Somosierra*, which would deal with the evolution of
Laforgue—and in other words, would presumably return to
and re-explore the same period as that dealt with in *Le Cheval
de Troie*—might well have proved to be a kind of
counterbalance. But given the wider concerns of *La
Conspiration*, it seems likely that Nizan, had he lived, would
have moved away from politically or ideologically driven
novels to ones in which philosophical issues would dominate,
and which would place him alongside Camus as one of the
major existentialist writers of the mid twentieth century.
Stylistically, too, it seems that he had now escaped the
prescriptions of socialist-realist theory and would continue to
refine the kind of variation and experimentation already
apparent in *La Conspiration*. But before that, his last published
novel had already made its mark. A number of contemporary
reviewers observed that it had its place in a series of novels
which already included Flaubert's *L'Éducation sentimentale*,
Barrès's *Les Déracinés* and Gide's *Les Faux-Monnayeurs*—
examples of the *Bildungsroman*, therefore—charting the
evolution and formative experiences of an individual or of a
group of young people. In many respects this is clearly the case,
but what distinguishes *La Conspiration* is the way in which
Nizan is constantly asking questions of and issuing a challenge
to his characters, himself and, above all, his readers. To the
end, Nizan remained 'responsible'.

Bibliography

The place of publication for works written in French, unless it is indicated to the contrary, is Paris.

Principal works by Nizan

Aden Arabie. Rieder, 1932.
(reissued with a preface by J.-P. Sartre, Maspero, 1960).

Les Chiens de garde. Rieder, 1932.

Antoine Bloyé. Grasset, 1933.

Le Cheval de Troie. Gallimard, 1935.

Les Matérialistes de l'antiquité.
Éditions sociales internationales, 1938.

La Conspiration. Gallimard, 1938.

Chronique de septembre. Gallimard, 1939.

See also:

Brochier, Jean-Jacques, *Paul Nizan, intellectuel communiste, écrits et correspondance 1926-1940.* Maspero, 1967.

Pour une nouvelle culture. Textes réunis et présentés par Susan Suleiman. Grasset, 1971.

Works on writers and the Communist party

Bernard, Jean-Pierre Arthur, *Le Parti Communiste français et la question littéraire, 1921-1939.* Presses Universitaires de Grenoble, 1972.

Caute, David, *Communism and the French Intellectuals.* London, André Deutsch, 1964.

Flower, John E., *Literature and the Left in France*. London, Macmillan, 1983 (reprinted London, Methuen, 1985).

Critical studies of Nizan

Alluin, Bernard & Deguy, Jacques (eds.), *Paul Nizan écrivain*, Actes du colloque des 11 et 12 décembre 1987. Presses Universitaires de Lille, 1988.

Arpin, Maurice, *La Fortune littéraire de Paul Nizan*. Berne, P. Lang («Publications universitaires européennes»), 1995.

Cohen-Solal, Annie & Nizan, Henriette, *Paul Nizan, communiste impossible*. Grasset, 1980.

Ginsbourg, Alain, *Nizan*. Éditions universitaires («Classiques du XXe siècle»), 1966.

Ishaghpour, Youssef, *Paul Nizan: une figure mythique de son temps*. Le Sycomore, 1980.

King, Adèle, *Paul Nizan, écrivain*. Didier, 1976.

Leiner, Jacqueline, *Le Destin littéraire de Paul Nizan et ses étapes successives: contribution à l'étude du mouvement littéraire en France de 1920 à 1940*. Klincksieck, 1970.

Ory, Pascal, *Nizan, Destin d'un révolté*. Ramsay, 1980.

Redfern, Walter, *Paul Nizan: Committed Literature in a Conspiratorial World*. Princeton University Press, 1972.

Scriven, Michael, *Paul Nizan: Communist Novelist*, Basingstoke, The Macmillan Press, 1988.

Steel, James, *Paul Nizan: un révolutionnaire conformiste?* Presses de la fondation nationale des sciences politiques, 1987.

See also:

Atoll , 1 (November / December 1967-January 1968).

Europe, nos. 784-785 (August-September 1994).